The WEALTH CENTER

Lisa Lee Hairston

ISBN: 978-1-4269-6018-5 (sc)
ISBN: 978-1-4269-6017-8 (e)

Trafford rev. 01/07/2012

 www.trafford.com

North America & international
toll-free: 1 888 232 4444 (USA & Canada)
phone: 250 383 6864 ✦ fax: 812 355 4082

Table of Contents

Dedication vii

Acknowledgements ix

Foreword xiii

Chapter One	The Wealth Center's Invitation	1
Chapter Two	The Limo	10
Chapter Three	The Wealth Center	18
Chapter Four	The Final Weekend At Home	34
Chapter Five	The Name Selection	37
Chapter Six	The Wealth Training	41
Chapter Seven	The Chapel Services	46
Chapter Eight	The Awakening	60
Chapter Nine	The First Bible Study	64
Chapter Ten	The Lamaze Room	72
Chapter Eleven	Lisa's First Place	79
Chapter Twelve	The Phenomenal Women's Conference	85
Chapter Thirteen	The Romantic Picnic For Two	112

Chapter Fourteen   The Thanksgiving Dinner   116

Chapter Fifteen   The Birthing Room   123

Chapter Sixteen   Lisa's Individualized
Education Plan (I.E.P.)   128

Chapter Seventeen   The More Perfect Union   134

Epilogue   141

Dedication

I would like to dedicate this book, *The Wealth Center*, first and foremost, to my God – The God of Abraham, Isaac and Jacob – the one who is absolutely the Source of all Wealth. He is without a doubt The Wealth Center in all of us!

Secondly, I dedicate this book to the late Thomas Jefferson Harbor and his beloved wife, Anna Lee Dalton Harbor, their family and extended family, as well as to the Simmons family.

A special thanks to my mother, Mary Lee Dalton Hairston; my brother, Anthony Jay Hairston; his wife, Diane Simmons Hairston; and my aunt, Jessie Maud Harbor.

Your presence in my life inspired this book. May God richly bless you!!!

Acknowledgements

I would like to extend a special thanks to Clintonia Wallace, Shamellow Lowe, Leander Mckenzie, Michelle Chatman, and Jewel Jerome Ziglar for their major contributions to this book. Without them, perhaps I would not have finished the book.

I would also like to extend an extra special thanks to Jose Romero, Lea Henry, Geda Ross, Nikia Corrales, Anna Mills, Edwin Ingram, and Kyle Anderson - the Trafford Publishing staff that I conferred with frequently throughout this process to make this book an absolute success! To all of you, a zillion thanks for making my first and second publishing process a pure joy!

This must be what paradise is made of. I look forward to working with you in my next two projects! May we all have a publishing relationship that will last for eternity!

All of the Bible Scriptures mentioned throughout this book are taken solely from the King James Version, unless otherwise noted!

Foreword

Acquiring the level of Infinite Wealth that Mary, Jason, and their unborn daughter, Lisa, achieved in this short novel, *The Wealth Center*, required a lot of diligence and time on their part, as well as on the part of The Wealth Center Staff, who went out of their way to make that Wealth possible.

Personally, you may or may not have that amount of time right now to spend in programming your own subconscious mind for wealth or the mind of someone you love. Trust me, I understand the concept: "Time is money, and money is time." If you waste a person's time, you waste his or her opportunity to make a substantial amount of money. And if you waste a person's potential to make lots of money, you diminish that person's quality and quantity of life that he or she will never be able to recapture unless he or she can make up for lost time.

For that reason, I have taken the liberty throughout this book to deliberately and intentionally capitalize, italicize, and or underline certain words, names, and phrases that will highly maximize your subconscious mind's capacity to absorb each word quickly to achieve your desired result in less time.

Please be advised that as I was typing this manuscript with all the words in its naturally, pure form (no capitalizations, etcetera), the infinite wealth I was writing about impressed my mind with so much wealth so quickly until I became frustrated with anything less than what I was reading about. I felt as though I was operating in some kind of "Godspeed" while others were functioning at a snail's pace.

Subsequently, I had no other choice but to read and re-read every single word in The Wealth Center every single day to make sure no one caused me to lose time focusing on anything but the Infinite Wealth that is naturally and supernaturally surrounding us all twenty-four hours a day, seven days a week, three hundred and sixty-five days of the year. As a result, I made the decision to capitalize and emphasize in some way all the words in this book that I feel is guaranteed to bypass your own conscious thinking process to get deep into your Spirit and your subconscious mind lightning fast, with Godspeed unheard of by the world.

At this point, as I went back to read the final draft before submitting it to my publisher, I considered what English majors and the educated sect would think when they initially read the words on each page. Yes, it is highly important to be grammatically correct, but in this case, when so many individuals are highly displeased about what is wrong with the economy, the high price of gasoline, and what the government is or is not doing to fix those problems, I would much rather be Spiritually correct.

If we all could capture the real essence and the true meaning of what this short Novel, *The Wealth Center*, is all about, and take the time each day to work this system (Biblical Meditation, and Subliminal Programming), I believe our voice would not only count, but would yield real and radical change we all could live with, regardless of our party affiliation. Is that not what we all want?

It is amazing to me that so many individuals will talk about what is not working in our country and abroad, but when push comes to shove, they would much rather call what could work, if put into practice, a fairytale. All day long, every day of the week, we all are a total sum of our own personal self-talk (what we say to ourselves and about ourselves and everything and everyone around us). This book is all about what it would be like to live exclusively in God's Economy that is void of our problems, lack, and limited point of view.

In this book, I wrote from both the prospective and the perspective of what our lives would be like if we acquired the same level of wealth that the characters in the novel did. They are no different than you or I, yet, when given the chance they capitalized on the opportunity presented to them. Of a truth, the fact that this book is in your hand is an indication that you, yourself, have been given an invaluable opportunity!!!

Approach this book with the right mindset, and you too, could have a life-transforming moment just reading the words on each page. Who knows what will happen when your psyche catches hold of these principles and act on them? But one thing is certain. By the time you will have finished reading this book, you should have come to the conclusion that true wealth is whatever you define it to be, and that anything is possible if we all change the way we think, or re-think what we think we already know.

Chapter One

THE WEALTH CENTER'S INVITATION

It was a gorgeous and beautiful day outside, but Mary was too deep in her own thoughts to notice. She was in a daze. One minute, she had been standing in the employment line seeking a job, and the next minute, she was sitting in the emergency room due to collapsing under the pressure and strain of trying to find work for the last six months.

"Congratulations, Mary," Dr. Scott said. "You are going to have a child. Go home and try to get some rest. I will have my secretary telephone you next week to set up an appointment with Dr. Cornelia Lee, an OB-GYN at the *New Childbirth Center* on Main Street. Do not worry about a thing. You are going to be all right."

Did Mary notice a tone in the last comment? There was a certain emphasis on "You are going to be all right?" Was Mary missing something, or were Dr. Scott's words hinting at something that was to come? Mary really could not think right now!!! She was going to have a child.

As Mary walked to the bus stop, which was only two minutes down the street, she wondered what Jason would say about the arrival of a new baby. They had just gotten married seven months ago, and they had been struggling financially. They were not financially prepared for this new bundle of joy. They had a few dollars in savings, but what was that compared to the cost of rearing a new child?

Mary did the only thing she could do at the moment. She would rest like the doctor ordered, starting with the long bus ride home. There would be plenty of time to break the news to Jason when he arrived home later tonight from the art gallery where he worked.

"Thank God that Jason was open to the idea of being a proud father," Mary sighed, with relief. He was more understanding than she thought he would be. "This baby is a gift from God, Mary!!! God will provide," Jason said. "He always has, and He always will."

True to Dr. Scott's word, *The New Childbirth Center* contacted Mary and Jason on the following week. They were scheduled to attend their first meeting on the 19th of January. During this time,

Mary and Jason would learn the gender of their child, or so they thought. They had gone online on their personal computer to a website where they learned that there was a new technology available for anyone who wanted to take a first look at their child.

Shockingly, Jason was more excited about their appointment than Mary was. As long as she had known Jason, he was the more intuitive of the two. He seemed to have a sixth sense about everything. "Did Jason know something about this pregnancy that she did not know?" Mary wondered. She would just have to wait and see!

Mary and Jason arrived at *The New Childbirth Center* on time, but due to an unexpected delivery at the hospital, Dr. Lee was running an hour late. Mary became anxious and agitated. After all, patience was not her greatest virtue. Often she had joked with Jason, saying, "When God was handing out patience, I was at the soda machine buying a Pepsi."

The longer Mary waited for the doctor to arrive, the more she felt she was being forced to think about things she did not want to deal with right now – thoughts of how she and Jason would provide for the baby that was now on the way. Mary was feeling somewhat skeptical about becoming a new mom.

Jason, on the other hand, was calm as he could be. He was an artist by profession, and he was admiring the office's Relaxing and delightfully Rich, warm, eye-catchingly, beautiful décor. Seeing the antique furnishings, the Rich, decadent, mahogany tables, the fabulously shiny mirrors, and the solid crystal chandeliers made Jason think the Seven Wonders of the World were nothing compared to what he was beholding at the present moment. If "beauty is in the eye of the beholder" as people say, "then Wealth must not be an exception either," Jason thought.

Wealth is in the eye of the one Beholding it, and wow was Jason Beholding and Taking In All Of That Wealth. Jason silently thanked his art professor for teaching him the value of capturing the essence of beauty on every artistic plane known to man. "Someday, all that brilliance will pay off," Jason thought to himself. "How, he did not know. "But, one day...."

After soaking in the Richness of the Room and Absorbing All Its Wealth, Jason stared calmly at some of the other families that were in the room. One man in particular captured his attention. Sitting across from him was an elderly man who was obviously enjoying reading *The Wall Street Journal.*

"Hello, my good man! My name is Ingram – Ingram Goodrich. Do you subscribe to the Wall Street Journal by any chance?" Jason quickly replied, "No, actually I do not. The thought never crossed my mind!" "What line of work are you in, son, if you do not mind me asking?" "I am an artist by profession," Jason said most emphatically. "In my opinion, you should try reading *The Wall*

Street Journal every day. Years ago, my father told me that if I read *The Wall Street Journal* every day, I would be Wealthy a Zillion times over. He was right!!! Would you like to take a shot at it? You might just need it to Increase Your Money Flow in the art industry."

To appease the man, Jason took *The Wall Street Journal* and began to skim through its pages, but not before noticing the vast array of magazines strategically placed on the Hefty and Luxurious table: *Fortune* Magazine, *Forbes* Magazine, the *Money* Magazine, *Parents* Magazine, *American Baby* Magazine, *Fit Pregnancy* Magazine, *Parent and Child* Magazine, *Parenting Early Years* Magazine, *Parenting School Years* Magazine, *Pregnancy & Newborn* Magazine, *Scientific American* Magazine, *Scientific American Mind* Magazine, *Health* Magazine, *Natural Health* Magazine, and the Yoga Journal.

Dr. Lee was now two hours late. Mary was about to jump out of her skin. "Sure enough, babies seem to be born on their own timetable," Mary thought impatiently, "but how much longer would the doctor be?" Just as Mary was about to get out of her chair to walk across the room to the receptionist's desk to inquire how much longer it would be before the doctor arrived, a young man, who appeared to be in his early 40's, approached the two of them.

He handed them both a business card. He said, "Hello, this may be hard to believe right now, but I am Dr. Lemar Rich. I am not a medical doctor as my name implies. I am a Wealth Specialist at The Wealth Center, which is located two hours away in the City of Chicago. Believe it or not, your baby has been chosen by The Wealth Center to participate in a life-long Wealth Mentorship Program. If you do not mind, I would love to chat with you about our program and why your family was selected by The Wealth Center."

Dr. Rich went on to ask, "Today, after your appointment with the doctor, do you have a few hours to accompany me to The Wealth Center where we would have more privacy to discuss this matter more fully?"

Mary was the first to speak up, "I am sorry. We do not know you. What could you possibly have to say to us?" Jason remained silent, but he was obviously open to what this Wealth Specialist had to say. He was beginning to wonder if this had anything to do with the man who had offered him *The Wall Street Journal.*

Lamar said, "I can understand your reaction to me. I am a stranger to you, but I am not a stranger to Dr. Lee. Once a year, Dr. Lee allows me to come to this office informally to observe, off the record, all the mothers who come to the office for their first doctor's visit. Without saying a word to the doctor or anyone, I make a decision as to which mothers may or may not be suitable for our Wealth Study.

If I feel, just by observation only, that a mother is a potential candidate for our program, I will approach her and identify myself. If she and her husband agree to meet with me, and they accept the terms of our program, they sign a medical release form, releasing Dr. Lee of any possible breach of patient and doctor confidentiality. I merely come here, as I said, once a year, only to observe the mothers who come in and out of the office. No medical information is transferred between Dr. Lee and me until the appropriate documents are signed. Therefore, there is never a breach of confidentiality. Should the proud parents- to-be say, "No," to my offer, nothing has been gained or lost by either party.

Only seven babies a year are selected to participate in our Life-Long Study, and I, a representative of The Wealth Center, feel that you and your baby are a perfect match for our program. I promise you that if you will give me a few hours of your time today after your appointment, you will better understand how this opportunity can and will change your life forever!"

At that moment, a nurse opened the door to call Mary and Jason back to the examination room. Dr. Lee had just arrived. As Mary and Jason walked towards the nurse, it was Jason who gave a backwards glance at Dr. Rich. Though he said nothing, something in Jason's eyes were begging Dr. Rich not to leave the office without them.

Meanwhile, Jason and Mary learned that it was much too early to discover the sex of their little one. Mary was only in the first trimester of her pregnancy, and not yet in the 7th week of her term. They would have to wait until at least the first week in Mary's second trimester, no earlier than the 14th week, before anyone would know for sure if she were having a girl or boy. But, what was known was that Mary was to give birth to her child on Friday, October 13th, the greatest day of the year. Why was it so great? Jason may have been the more intuitive of them, but neither of them believed in silly superstitions or bad luck. Mary and Jason were having their first child. What was unlucky about that?

As Mary and Jason exited the examination room, Jason was obviously overjoyed. You would think that the baby had already arrived. Jason was like a man handing out cigars on the day of delivery. Mary's thoughts were interrupted as she heard Dr. Lee say, "I hear that there is a Dr. Rich in the front lobby who would love to talk to you. Is that correct?" "Yes," said Jason, nervously. Jason knew his wife better than anyone and he knew she did not want to speak to anyone at the Wealth Center.

He was right. Mary said, "We must hurry if we are going to catch the next bus. If we miss it, we will have to wait at least an extra hour." Dr. Rich said, "Mary and Jason, my car is waiting outside if you would still like to accompany me to the Wealth Center. We can leave right now if you want. It is only a two-hour drive. Of course, if you choose not to take me up on my offer, I would still be more than happy to have my driver drive you home."

At that moment, a long, white stretch limousine pulled up at the door, and a chauffeur got out of it to open the door for Dr. Rich. The chauffeur asked, "Will the proud parents be joining us this morning, Dr. Rich?" Mary and Jason looked at one another in both bewilderment and amazement.

"Who was this man that would come to the doctor's office in a limo just to talk to them," they thought? Mary said, "I guess we could spare a couple of hours. We do not have anything else to do!!!" But, Jason could still feel his wife's apprehension. She looked flustered.

Chapter Two

THE LIMO

Inside the limo, Mary and Jason were astonished at what they were seeing. Neither of them had been in a limo before – not even on their wedding day. They could not afford it. That is why Mary and Jason were still riding the bus. They were trying to save as much money as they possibly could. It was Jason who believed that things would get better for them Financially. He was tired of worrying about how they could make ends meet. "He would think about that later," he thought.

Everything about this car reeked with Wealth. There was a pantry well stocked with Perrier, cheese, shrimp, caviar, ordeurves, finger foods, fruit, orange juice, milk, crackers, and everything that was healthy for a pregnant woman to eat and drink.

This was more food than what Mary and Jason were used to. There was very little food in their refrigerator at the present moment. Just when Mary started to fret about providing for their baby, Dr. Rich said, "Do not be frightened. Enjoy what the Wealth Center has provided for you today. It is a Prelude to Even More Wealth."

Mary and Jason did not need a second invitation to enjoy the feast set before them. They ate to their heart's content. They had not seen this much food in months. Life had been a struggle for them with Mary being unemployed. That is how she had ended up in the emergency room in the first place. She had collapsed when she could not find work.

Mary had practically spent all her life after high school pursuing one college degree after another. She had hoped to get a Ph.D in something, though she had no idea in what area of expertise. She had wanted to be a District Attorney, but she could never see herself winning an election. She had wanted to, at one time, specialize in criminal law. She would have made an excellent attorney, but she never believed that she would attract any clients. Mary's dream job was to serve her country as a Senator, but she doubted her own potential. She had also wanted to be a psychiatrist, but she definitely did not want to go to medical school.

Mary spent many years working in lower-paying jobs. She had worked in fast food briefly, but she was not cut out for that kind of work. She obviously had a passion for catering, but she could not handle the long hours. If only Mary could find herself! Mary felt like such a failure. She was not the only one who felt that way. Many of her family members and friends felt the same way, too. Thank heavens for Jason who never once complained. He loved her dearly. She was the Love Of His Life. He saw the best in her, when she and no one else did not. "If only she could do better," Mary thought.

Dr. Rich was smiling from ear to ear as he happily watched Mary and Jason enjoy the delicacies they were now eating. He had been here before. He knew that these parents, just like all the other parents who had preceded them on this particular ride, were with each bite, feeling the Luxury, the Wealth, the Richness, and Unlimited Abundance that so many people enjoy but so many others do not. He knew that this Feeling and Atmosphere of Wealth would <u>Empower</u> Mary and Jason to make the right decision about the offer he would soon make them. To date, only one other couple had rejected Dr. Rich's offer to participate in the Wealth Center Study, and they had been right in the decision they had made.

That family was an excellent candidate for the program, but only a couple can decide if they are willing to take the time everyday to Meditate On Wealth. The husband and wife team were not willing to put in the time necessary to Attracting Wealth on an Astronomical Scale. Dr. Rich had been in this business for what seemed like an eternity, and he knew that Mary and Jason were different. They wanted to give their baby the best in life, though they were not experiencing the best right now. But they would experience it because of their hunger for something better!

In the limo, there was not a lot of idle chit chat. There really was not time for that. Mary and Jason were deep in thought. They were Absorbing the Wealth they were encountering. They were obviously enjoying the classical music. Dr. Rich had deliberately chosen Mozart and Beethoven's musical compositions as a backdrop to be softly heard in the background. He had also carefully chosen several Bach Cantatas. Such music not only can help alter one's mood, it can also aid in developing language development, spatial reasonings, and thought processes.

Mary and Jason listened attentively as Dr. Rich told them a few stories about classical music. This was one of the rare moments when Dr. Rich chose to speak. This was part of the Wealth Training that the Wealth Center provided. It was important for Mary and Jason to know how classical music could be beneficial to both them and their baby.

For example, Mary and Jason did not know that listening to classical music could change one's mood, and make one to Relax. They did not know that classical music would affect their baby. Jason had an ear and eye for art, not for classical music. But, there was never a day that went by that Mary and Jason were not listening to Rhythm and Blues. A house is not a home if there is not the right music playing in the home daily. That was

Jason's philosophy. They found listening to music Relaxing, if not Romantic. They had never given a thought, however, to listening to classical music.

In addition to listening to the classical music, Mary and Jason also had access to the Subliminal Wealth Tapes that were also playing in the background when the music was not playing. The ride to the Wealth Center was indeed two hours, so there was plenty of time to listen to everything that was available. It did not take a genius to figure out that the Tapes were working. In the short time that Mary and Jason were in the limo, their Subconscious Mind was Absolutely Receiving The Wealth Programming. Once they started to believe that Having Wealth and Being Wealthy was their God-Given Heritage, they could never and would never go back to a mundane, mediocre, and under-privileged lifestyle. These were the words that Mary and Jason heard on the Tape:

"Today is the first day of the rest of your life. This is not the end. It is just the beginning of your walking out of poverty, poor thinking, and meager living and stepping into the lifestyles of the Rich, Wealthy, and Happy.

I hope you are sitting down right now, because for the next thirty minutes or so, I am going to expose you to a level of your God-Given Wealth that is so Uncommon, so amazing, so powerful, and so Astronomical, it will literally blow your mind.

Having Wealth is your God-Given Right. Having Wealth is your Highest Calling. Having Wealth is your Destiny. Having Wealth is your Lot in Life. And Having Wealth is Your Station in Life. It is your time to move from Last Class to First Class. If you will dare to believe that all the Wealth in the Universe from Adam and Eve up to now is yours, there is no limit to how Wealthy you can and will become.

Most people, especially those who know you best, will try to convince you that Being Wealthy is not for you – that Having Unlimited Wealth is only a Fairytale, and does not exist in the real world. Nothing could be both further and farther from the truth!

What is the Truth? What is the Real Reality? The Real Reality – The Real Truth is that living in lack, and living in a state of poverty where there is never enough - where you are just barely making it from pay check to paycheck is the Fairytale

<u>In God, In Christ, and In the Holy Ghost, there is Wealth that has yet to be tapped into! There is Wealth that has yet to Begotten</u>. Having Wealth is Biblical! Having More Than Enough is Biblical! Having a Lot is Biblical! Having an Abundance of Wealth is Biblical! Living Wealthy is Biblical! And Living as an Ambassador of Wealth is Biblical. Anything less than that is unreal. Anything that is not Biblical is not God's Will.

It is God's Will for you to be Wealthy, and to Live In Wealth second by second, minute by minute, hour by hour, day by day, week by week, month by month, year by year, as long as you live. You have been chosen to be Exposed to all the Wealth that God ordained for you from the foundations of the world. Be Warned: This kind of Wealth is not for the faint of heart or for unbelievers who cannot and will not believe this Wealth exists. It is only designed for those who are not afraid to be a demonstration of that Wealth. It is only for those who do not feel the need to apologize to anyone for Having Wealth. One should never be sorry for Having Wealth!!!

It is as NATURAL for you to Have Wealth as it is for fish to live in water! What happens, by the way, if you take a fish out of the water it was created to live in? It will die because it was not intended to live anywhere but in the Environment and Atmosphere it was Created to be in. On the same token, you cannot and will not survive outside of your Wealthy Atmosphere and Wealthy Environment. Why? It is not your Natural Habitat!!!

There may be many critics to Wealth, but just know that those critics are either not Wealthy, or they do not want to see you Acquire Wealth. In any case, if you choose to listen to them, they will absolutely and indisputably talk you out of the Wealth they already know is yours. Who will you choose to believe - the doomsayers - the naysayers - the soothsayers? Or will you believe that Wealth is your destiny? The choice is yours – and yours alone!!! Be it done to you according to your faith!

Believe the Wealth! See the Wealth! Hear the Wealth! Smell the Wealth! Taste the Wealth! Touch the Wealth! That Wealth is just as real as the air you breathe each day. <u>You, my friend, are not going to become Wealthy!!! You are already Wealthy!!! In fact, you were born Wealthy when you were born into a Wealthy Universe that God Himself Spoke Into Existence!!! You, my friend, have that same speaking power!!!</u>"

Mary and Jason had never heard of anything like this. No one had ever taken the time to talk them about Money, Finances or Wealth. But, none of that mattered. They were hearing it now!!! And they were Believers!!!! This was only the first of many Wealth Tapes that they would have access to.

Chapter Three

THE WEALTH CENTER

As exquisite as the food pantry in the limo was, it had nothing on how Grandiose The Wealth Center was. The buildings that stood larger than life on the twelve-acre campus were so Phenomenally Wealthy-Looking until Mary and Jason almost lost their breath temporarily looking at such an Extravagant display. There was not a house around in either direction for twenty miles. The landscape was so beautiful, one would have thought he or she had died and went to Heaven.

Every square inch of The Wealth Center - the Grounds and the Estate - looked Wealthy beyond anyone's human intellect or understanding. No human words could describe the Opulence Mary and Jason were beholding. The Buildings itself looked like they had been built by a <u>Zillionaire</u>.

And Mary and Jason should know a thing or two about these sorts of things. After all, they lived in Lake Geneva, Wisconsin - a place that was known for its beautiful landscapes, homes, and tourist attractions. Initially, Mary had not wanted to live here in what she considered the Midwest, approximately 910 miles away from the place she had lived in all her life. She was a northern girl from Kennebunkport, Maine, a place that was Rich in tradition and history. By nature, Mary was a loner, if not a recluse, and during the summer months, she had enjoyed going to Goose Rocks Beach many times just to settle down with a good book. It was quiet there, and Mary could think about her future. Of course, she wondered if she could ever have one.

In Kennebunkport, Maine, the majority of employees were white-collar workers, and the average income was just over $50,000. Is it any wonder that Mary had fainted while at the employment office! Mary's surroundings had not rubbed off on her, and unfortunately, Mary could just never seem to get ahead, no matter how hard she tried. No one in her family could ever understand why she could never seem to excel at anything. Life for her in Lake Geneva, Wisconsin was no different. Jason had talked Mary into moving to Wisconsin to live after they were married. He had hoped Mary would find herself there. But, for some reason or another, Mary just did not seem to fit in.

Jason had been attracted to this area because it was an <u>Excellent Opportunity</u> for him to get in touch with his right-brained nature. He and his family felt that his artistic ability in such an amazing town would pay off for him and Mary Financially. Jason could get lost capturing on canvas All The Wealth his eyes could see. After all, Jason had fallen in love with this place after he received his Bachelor's degree in Fine Arts from one of the finest art schools in the country. It was the least his family could do for him to try to help him Get On His Feet Financially and get established in the art industry. Perhaps this was as close to Wealth as Jason could possibly get. No one knew for sure! Only time would tell.

For one brief moment, as Mary took in such amazing Luxury, her mind went back to a sermon she had heard during a church service in Kennebunkport, Maine many years ago. The minister had read the passage of scripture from Revelation 21:10-21:

"And he carried me away in the spirit to a great and high mountain, and shewed me that great city, the holy Jerusalem, descending out of heaven from God. Having the glory of God: and her light was like unto a stone most precious, even like a jasper stone, clear as crystal: And had a wall great and high, and had twelve gates, and at the gates twelve angels, and names written thereon, which are the names of the twelve tribes of the children of Israel. On the east three gates; on the north three gates; on the south three gates; and on the west three gates. And the wall of the city had twelve foundations, and in them the names of the twelve apostles of the Lamb. And he that talked with me had a golden reed to measure the city, and the gates thereof, and the wall thereof. And the city lieth foursquare, and the length is as large as the breadth: and he measured the city with the reed, twelve thousand furlongs. The length and the breadth and the height of it are equal. And he measured the wall thereof, an hundred and forty and four cubits, according to the measure of a man, that is, of the angel. And the building of the wall of it was of jasper: and the city was pure gold, like unto clear glass. And the foundations of the wall of the city were garnished with all manner of precious stones. The first foundation was jasper; the second, sapphire, the third, a chalcedony; the fourth, an emerald; the fifth, sardonyx, the sixth, sardius, the seventh, chrysolyte; the eighth, beryl; the ninth, a topaz, the tenth, a chrysoprasus, the eleventh, a jacinth, the twelfth, an amethyst. And the twelve gates were twelve pearls; every several gate was of one pearl: and the street of the city was pure gold, as it were transparent glass..."

Mary and Jason were absolutely awestruck, not to mention speechless! Mary was in tears. "Was this a dream?" "Was this a fantasy?" They had never seen anything this Wealthy or Brilliant! And they had yet to step foot on the Inside of The Wealth Center Lobby or on the Inside of any of the other Buildings, for that matter.

Could their heart take the Wealth they would see when they stepped into The Wealth Center's Lobby? What about the other Buildings they had yet to step foot in? Mary and Jason felt as if the whole Campus were one complete City within itself. One would think they were in the City of Heaven – a City more dazzling than anything anyone at anytime had ever seen. Mary and Jason could see why someone would name this place The Wealth Center. Wealth was truly the center, if not the forefront, of this Phenomenal Estate. This place – The Wealth Center - was not Heaven, but it was as close as it gets!

As Mary and Jason entered the Main Lobby, they noticed they had stepped across a plush red carpet. The Wealth Center had gone out of its way to give Mary and Jason the illusion that they had just rolled out the red carpet for them, and only them. This strategy was working! Mary felt like a famous celebrity who had just won an Oscar!

Yes, Mary and Jason could and did stand what they saw when their eyes beheld the Lavish and Luxurious Interior of The Wealth Center's Lobby. The Interior of the Lobby was equally as Wealthy as the Exterior of the Building. They could not wait to see the other Buildings first hand and up close!

Mary and Jason got it immediately!!!! They understood that there can only be Outer Wealth if the Inner Wealth is present. Real Wealth - True Wealth - starts from the Inside Out, not from the Outside In. If you are Wealthy on the Inside, then Wealth – External Wealth - Will Materialize Automatically!!! Once you get Wealthy on the Inside, no Outer Circumstance can prevent that Wealth from coming forth. Absolutely nothing!!! And that is exactly what The Wealth Center would do for Mary and Jason's child, if permitted.

There were a slew of Wealth Trainers, Wealth Specialists, and Wealth Center staff on hand to give Mary and Jason a royal tour of the entire Campus. But, Dr. Rich did the honors himself. <u>There was too much at stake</u>.

The process of The Wealth Center Study had begun the very minute Dr. Rich laid eyes on Mary the day she had visited Dr. Lee's office. "One wrong step, thought Dr. Rich, and Mary and Jason could fail to comprehend the True Nature of the Wealth Study. Every word and every question spoken by Dr. Rich must lead this <u>Happy Couple</u> to say yes to life-long Wealth. The Tapes Mary and Jason had listened to in the limo were only one part of the process."

Each Room of every Building that Mary and Jason entered mesmerized them. Every Piece of Furniture, every Square Inch of red carpeting at each Door's Entrance (chosen to make one feel as though he or she was walking down the red carpet), and every Accessory had been carefully selected to Create an Atmosphere of Wealth. It was important that each person Feel the Wealth! Wow, were Mary and Jason feeling the Wealth!

Even the Dining Room looked Wealthy enough for the Wealthiest King to enjoy. Being a female, Mary Appreciated the Mood of the Room that was Deliberately Accentuated by the ponytail brown and the pearl white interior. Each time Mary stepped into this part of the Wing, she felt like a beautiful princess, not to mention the Queen of her castle. "At some point, Mary thought, she would try her hand at interior decorating." She would talk to The Wealth Center staff about that urgent matter later. Jason could not be more pleased!!!

They even had a Wealthy-Looking State of the Art Lamaze Class for the proud parents to be. Over the Lamaze Class door were these words from the Bible, which were strategically placed throughout the Campus, including The Wealth Center's Entrance: "Beloved, I wish above all things that thou mayest prosper and be in health, even as thy soul prospers" (3 John 2).

Dr. Lamar Rich did not want to get too far ahead of himself by giving away more information about the Lamaze Class. It was unlike any other Class in the world – all of which he would explain later if Mary and Jason offered his Proposal. First, they would have to decide if <u>their child would participate in the Wealth Study</u>.

Once inside Dr. Rich's Office, he got down to the business of Revealing more about The Wealth Center's Mission. "Mary and Jason, said Dr. Rich, you have been chosen by The Wealth Center to participate in a Life-Long Wealth Study. The Wealth Center <u>Specializes</u> in Wealth that is based solely on Biblical Principles and Scriptures, especially the one in Proverbs 22:6: "Train up a child in the way that he should go, and when he is old, he shall not depart."

Years ago, the Founder of The Wealth Center, Dr. Joseph Winslow, in keeping with Proverbs

22:6, decided to conduct a Wealth Study, but only with women who had just found about their pregnancy. He would invite the mom and dad pair to live at The Wealth Center, and while here, he would provide the mother with <u>the Best Prenatal Care available</u>, but with a hitch.

During every visit to the OB-GYN that is on staff here, there would be classical music playing in the background, as well as an assortment of Wealth Tapes that could be heard in the examination room as well. The same goes for our Meditation Room, our Chapel, and in the dining areas during meals. In fact, from sunrise to sunset, Wealth Tapes can be heard from anywhere here on the site – whether indoors or outdoors.

During story time, mothers have the option of selecting which Wealth Stories they want to <u>read to their unborn child</u>. In every nursery, which is just off each family's master bedroom, you can see each mother rocking in her rocker as she and her child are Intentionally Programmed for Wealth. This same procedure of playing Subliminal Tapes and Soothing Music is carried out in the Birthing Room as well each time a mother gives birth to her beloved son or daughter."

Mary and Jason were eager to interrupt Dr. Rich with at least one million questions, but they kept silent instead. They were wondering what the Founder, Dr. Joseph Winslow, was expecting to accomplish or achieve during his Wealth Study. They would soon discover the answer.

Dr. Winslow, was not only an OB-GYN, he also possessed a strong, proven success record in Psychology, Research, and Child Development. <u>He wanted to see if the children who participated in the Wealth Study, first as Unborn Fetuses, then after Childbirth, were any better off Cognitively than children who were never a part of the Wealth Study. Dr. Winslow wanted to know if the children participating in the Wealth Study were predisposed to talking, acting, or behaving as if they had been born Wealthy. Would they or would they not think differently than other children who had not been Programmed for Wealth?</u>

"One hundred percent of all our participants, said Dr. Rich, did in fact think and behave differently than children who never came to The Wealth Center. Each girl and boy behaved as normally as peers their own age. For example, the girls still played with their Barbie dolls, and the boys still played with their Tonka trucks, and all children, both boys and girls had a great time riding their bikes and socializing with other children. But each child's mannerisms and conversations were different.

They all started their own businesses before they were teenagers and as a result, they all Acquired Massive Wealth. They conducted Leadership Classes to teach children outside The Wealth Center how to be Successful. They set High Goals and accomplished them all. They were also well respected by their peers. Though they were Successful on every level, they could all maintain a Healthy balance between work and play. They inspired children of all ages to excel Inside and Outside the Classroom.

That is why, Dr. Rich went on to say, you have been carefully selected to Participate in this Wealth Study. Upon the death of Dr. Winslow, he left us with a yearly Endowment of $100 Trillion, with specifications and conditions.

Each year, the seven families that agree to come to The Wealth Center and participate in the Wealth Study are given $1 Million a year Stipend for the rest of their lives. The Founder believed this was only a small token of what the Impact of this Research Study can have. Once this idea catches on, parents from all walks of life, especially the less than rich will want their child to have the same Advantage. All the Data that we have collected over the years – all of the Training Materials that we have used with Great Success Will Be At Everyone's Disposal so everyone can Learn How To Attract Wealth. Anybody, Anywhere can and will Benefit from this Wealth Study. You, my friends, are a part of that Great History and Heritage."

Lamar went on to say, "Should you decide to Participate in the Wealth Study, you would be expected to live here on Campus, effectively immediately. You may come and go as you please as you would if you were in the privacy of your own home. You would still be the parents of your beautiful child, with all your full parental rights intact. But, we alone would be solely responsible for all the Wealth Programming and Wealth

Training that your child would need for the rest of his or her natural life. Your child will never lack for anything. In addition to your Stipend, you will all have <u>The Best of Everything</u>! That comes with the territory. Most people would die to be in your position. But, you were chosen."

"Oh, and by the way, Lamar said quickly, did I mention that your child will also be allotted $5 Million a year for the rest of his or her natural life? That does not include all the Money he or she will Attract and Acquire Automatically on his or her own because he or she was Blessed with a Wealthy Mentality from his or her Mother's Womb? No one knows exactly how Wealthy your child will become as a result of being in our Wealth Study. But there is one thing that can be adequately predicted with 100% accuracy!

Having a Wealthy Mindset and a Wealthy Mentality will only Give Birth to More and More Wealth. Once that Wealth starts, no one, in here, or outside of these walls, can turn that Wealth off. <u>Your child will be the Wealthiest child in the world. Who would not want that for their son or daughter?</u> That is the beauty of the Wealth Center.

We can talk later about the extent of your son or daughter's Mandatory Training that we must provide as part of this Wealth Study. But, be assured, that here on this Campus, your child will be offered the Wealthiest Training available through his or her prenatal care, postnatal care, infancy, teenage years, as well as high school, throughout college, and beyond, for as long as you want it.

You can walk away from this Program at any moment, with all the Money we promised you, henceforth and forever. Moreover, <u>your Input as well as your Child's Input will always be welcome, encouraged, and incorporated into the program.</u>

As your child becomes older, and we have a sneaking suspicion that Mary will give birth to a daughter, you can choose to live Off Campus, if you wish, anywhere you wish. Should you go that route, we would assist you in choosing a perfectly suitable home in an Atmosphere, or should I say in a neighborhood that will promote Wealthy Thinking. We will always respect your privacy, and when necessary, we will step into the background, and allow all of you to enjoy your life without any strings attached. <u>Our main objective is to teach your child how to Think and Live Wealthy, Healthy, and Happy for the rest of his or her life, while at the same time ensuring that he or she has as close to a normal life as possible.</u> After all, play time is very instrumental in the healthy development of every child."

This was a life-changing moment for Mary and Jason. Their child would have the <u>Best of Everything</u>. He or she would be <u>Healthy, Wealthy, and Happy</u> just as God intended. The Wealth Center's only job would be to open up their child's heart and soul to all the Wealth that surrounded him or her. Mary and Jason's child would be Trained To See Wealth in places where other children, teenagers, and adults would not dream of looking. After all, that was the reason Dr. Winslow founded such a Great Wealth Establishment.

Not every child was born with a silver spoon in his or her mouth. At least that is what most people who have not yet tapped into Infinite Wealth Think. And not every parent has the Spiritual eye and savvy to Expose his or her child to Unlimited Wealth.

Practically every child has gone to sleep to a lullaby or a bedtime story such as Goldilocks and the Three Bears, and Hansel and Gretel, etcetera, but how many children have gone to sleep with <u>Visions of Becoming Wealthy</u>? <u>What if there were the kind of stories that could Condition all children to Think, Act, and Live Wealthy?</u> These kinds of Books, Books on Tape, CD's and DVD's are Housed in the Wealth Center's State of the Art Library.

Here at The Wealth Center, Mary and Jason's child would come to view having Great Wealth as being NATURAL. There are some adults who think it is wrong to be Wealthy or to even Think about being so. There are some people who do not think too highly of anyone who Possesses Astronomical Wealth. Some individuals do not want Wealth because they are content with their Financial Lot In Life.

True Wealth is having everything you need each day, without worrying how you will be provided for. But why settle for less than Great Wealth? Being that Wealthy is PLEASING to God!!! Why? The Universe is Full of Wealth that the world has yet to tap into. It would be a sin not to enjoy, experience, and share that Wealth. And soon, their child would have access to all that Wealth, beginning the very minute they moved into The Wealth Center. And Mary and Jason would benefit from all that Wealth Training as well, which really started the moment Lemar handed them his business card.

The choice was clear, at least to Jason. Without hesitation, Jason said, "As head of this family, I have decided that we will accept The Wealth Center's Offer. We Owe it to our child to give him or her the Best Head Start In Life." With tears in his eyes, Lamar said, "Great. We will make all the arrangements for you to move in immediately. You will not be sorry for making this decision!

Out of respect to you and Mary, please feel free to bring anything from home that might make you more comfortable – perhaps some keepsakes, favorite pictures, or any Antiques that are dear and precious to you. But, once you move in, our staff will Accommodate your every need. As you will soon discover, Money is not an object here. You will have lots of time to shop for anything you might want later.

So in the meantime, our chauffeur will drive you home, where you can enjoy the weekend. He will return to pick you up on Monday morning at

9:00 a.m. sharp. At that time, everything might seem a little hectic to you. Dr. Lee is also on staff here, and by the time of your return back to Campus, you will be in your second trimester, if not close to it, and he will be on hand to discover the sex of your unborn child, which I am sure you are very excited to learn. But, Dr. Lee is much more capable of advising you in those matters. <u>I am just a Wealth Specialist who happens to enjoy my task of working as a Team with the staff here to get you from Point A to Point B, effortlessly</u>.

Also on Monday, Dr. Lee will help plan your pre-natal care, your baby's Wealth Training, and he will also schedule appointments for you to meet the nutritionist and Lamaze Instructor. There will be lots and lots of questionnaires to be filled out by you, some initial interviews, and to help you to be more at ease, we will have an attorney of your own choosing on hand to review all the paper work.

May I add that you will have ample time to select a name for your baby? We will have a female on hand to expedite that process. She has about a million baby books on hand with names that you have never even dreamed of. Only you can choose the name of your child. But, you will find that as soon as you select a name, your baby's Wealth Training will be officially under way."

Mary said, "Why is our baby's name so important in the Wealth Training process?" Lamar said, "Great question, Mary?" "A person's name is like music to his or her ears. Your objective is to select <u>a name that Highly Symbolizes Wealth</u>. Every time you, I, a staff member, or anyone outside these walls speaks your child's name, he or she will <u>Feel Wealthy</u>. That is part of the Wealth Training."

As Mary and Jason sat in the limo, knowing they were about to spend the last weekend of their lives in their less than modest home, they were GRATEFUL for what they had just seen and heard. They Had Been Chosen for this new chapter in their lives, and they could not wait to turn the next page to see what would happen next!

Chapter Four

THE FINAL WEEKEND AT HOME

Mary and Jason exited the limo. They were so keyed up about the Wealthy Fate that had befallen them, they barely noticed the two-hour ride home. As they were unlocking the door to the home they had lived in for the last seven months, Paul, the chauffeur, handed them an envelope. There was a note inside which read: "Mary and Jason, you are about to embark upon a Wealthy Journey Beyond Your Wildest Dreams! During your final weekend in a home you love so dearly, we want you to <u>Create Wealthy Memories</u> that you will never forget! Please accept this $5,000 monetary gift to help you Celebrate your life together for the last seven months in any way that you wish. With Great Love, The Wealth Center!"

Enjoy, Mary and Jason did. They spent the rest of the night taking lots of pictures so they could show them to their child when he or she was old enough to understand how they all went from Rags to Riches. In addition, Mary and Jason rented a lot of movies to watch, after enjoying a Romantic, Candlelight Dinner For Two.

Moments after Paul had left, they took a leisurely stroll up the street to the all-night deli, and they purchased salmon steak, filet mignon, French bread, and all the ingredients they needed to make a lovely salad. For dessert, they chose a chocolate, raspberry cheesecake. Neither Mary or Jason drank alcohol, therefore, they unanimously decided to cap the evening off with a cold bottle of ginger ale. Thereafter, they spent the rest of the weekend enjoying their final moments of privacy.

Like clockwork, Paul, the chauffeur, arrived at their home on Monday at 9:00 a.m. on the dot. Mary and Jason did not have a lot of things to take with them to The Wealth Center. They had decided not to sell their home. They had, in good faith, given their house to a young, married couple that had just come back from their honeymoon in Hawaii. Jason had met Heirloom Wellington and his lovely wife, Chelsea, at the art gallery last year when he, himself, was sponsoring his first public art exhibit. He, Mary, and the Wellingtons had become great friends.

The Wellington's had agreed that they would live in the house rent-free, and would keep up the home in the best way they could. Mary and Jason would, from time to time, visit the home to check on how well the family was doing. In that way, their

child would always know where he or she was
<u>Conceived In Love</u>. The Wellington's could get
established and complete their doctorates as well.
Once the Wellington's completed their degrees,
they planned to move to the Virgin Islands to
begin their new teaching careers in Marine and
Environmental Science. "When that time came,"
Jason thought, "he and Mary would decide what
to do with their home – whether to sell it on the
market or keep it as a memory of how their lives
had changed for the better."

Mary and Jason took one long, last look at
their home. They had chosen to leave everything
behind except Mary's wedding dress, her wedding
album, her china, her Wealth Portfolio that she
had tried to use to motivate herself, her photo
album, and a shawl her mother had knitted for
her. Jason only brought along a Gold Watch which
belonged to his dad, his wedding tuxedo, his
photo album, and all of his paintings. He was after
all, an artist by profession.

In the limousine, the pantry was once again
well-stocked, but they ate lightly. Paul had
informed them that they would be having brunch
in their new home, The Wealth Center, with
Lamar, as soon as they arrived on campus. After
which, they would meet the rest of the staff. Better
yet, they would learn the sex of their child. How
exciting!!!!!!!!

Chapter Five

THE NAME SELECTION

Jason, Mary, and Lamar enjoyed a hearty meal that had been served in their new dining room, which was located on the East Wing. There was an assortment of breads, bagels, croissants, cream cheese, other delicious cheeses, fruit, Danishes, pastries, waffles, French toast, syrup, shrimp, grits, bacon, sausage, eggs, orange juice, and Perrier.

This breakfast was a long one. It lasted almost two hours. The purpose of this breakfast was to make Mary and Jason Feel Comfortable in their New Surroundings, and to help them to become Saturated with the Wealthy Atmosphere and Environment. It was important that the baby, mom and dad Feel the Wealth of their new home daily!

After breakfast, Mary and Jason were escorted to the doctor's office, which was located on the top floor of The Wealth Center to learn the sex of their child. The doctor had been right! They were having a girl! The baby would be due on Friday, October 13, 2011.

It is customary for some individuals, if not most, to believe that anyone born on the 13th of any month is unlucky. But Mary and Jason had just been offered a Dream Of A Lifetime. Their baby daughter would be born with every Possible Advantage in the world. Lisa would be provided with at least $5 Million a year for the rest of her life. What could possibly be unlucky about that?

After Mary and Jason learned they were to be proud parents of a baby daughter, they joined Dr. Rich in the nursery, which had yet to be decorated. This feat was to be undertaken by Mary and Jason. After all, they had been told upon their arrival that the Wealth Center was their home away from home and that they had full parental rights as if they were still living back home. It would be their right to select the color scheme of their new baby's room, as well as the rest of the décor anywhere in the house.

As Mary and Jason were eagerly taking in the Wealthy Atmosphere of the Room, Daphne appeared. With her were two other women who carried volumes of books containing baby names. It appeared as if Daphne did have one million books on hand. She needed to stress to Mary and Jason the importance of their baby girl's name. Daphne believed that as soon as a name was chosen, the Baby's Presence would be Felt throughout The Wealth Center. That is when the

Real Wealth Training would seem to come to life for everyone.

Daphne and her two assistants, Kelly and Samantha, did not stay in the nursery the whole time. They did not want to interfere with the selection of the baby's name. They only came in every hour or so to monitor Mary and Jason's progress in selecting a name for their new bundle of joy.

After spending at least three hours (not counting breaks in between) Mary and Jason selected a name for their precious daughter. After much deliberation, they decided to call their new precious bundle of joy, Lisa Lee Chancellor. What a Wealthy Name! It would be a Name that would be forever cherished by the delightfully, happy parents, the entire Wealth Center staff, and everyone who came into contact with amazing Lisa!!!

It might bear mentioning that the name Lisa is taken from the Hebrew name, Elizabeth, which means The Consecrated One – One who is Consecrated to God – God swore by an oath that He would Bless her. Lee, which is a name handed down from at least five successive generations on the mother's side, means "meadow."

For their baby girl, the name Lee would be thought of as "The Prosperous One." Lisa was not even born yet, and she was already proving to be More Than Prosperous! Mary and Jason were Christians who chose to Worship God on

Saturday rather than on Sunday, and during their first church appearance at The Wealth Center, they had heard the minister teaching on the Passage of Scripture found in Deuteronomy 28, which many believe to be the "Blessed chapter." At this point, Blessings seemed to be "overtaking them" by a landslide.

Mary and Jason were not prepared for what happened next. They were quickly ushered out to the south lawn only to see the entire staff waiting for them. Daphne was all teary eyed when she said, "Everyone is waiting to hear the name of your child. Please take the podium and make the announcement."

When Mary seemed to be a little shy, Jason took her by the hand and started walking quickly towards the platform. Very proudly, and loudly, Jason said, "Our daughter will be called Lisa Lee Chancellor." Music started playing in the background, cheers rang out, and a Wealth Center Flag was raised. Lisa's Wealth Training had just begun – From Her Mother's Womb!

After all the pomp and circumstance ended, May and Jason decided to take a nap in their new master suite. They had not been expecting this level of attention. They were not used to being in the spotlight. They had no idea How Serious everyone at The Wealth Center was about Saturating a person's life with Wealth – let alone their Lisa.

Chapter Six

THE WEALTH TRAINING

Mary and Jason dozed for a couple of hours before being awakened by a knock at the door. It was Dr. Lee. He was obviously beaming with joy. He had apparently already heard about the name selection. He had been at his other office when Mary and Jason made their exhilarating announcement on the south lawn.

He said, "I am not going to stay very long. I know today's Celebration took its toll on you, Mary, so I will be brief. I just brought along a schedule of your daily activities that pertain to your Prenatal Care, your Nutrition, your Lamaze Class, Lisa's Wealth Training, and Story Time, etcetera.

As you see, we will have a lot of work to do on certain days, if not every day, but there will be plenty of time for you and us to pamper all of you. I also brought some Reading Materials that you can personally read yourself to enhance your own Wealthy Mentality. I Have these books, which were published here by our Wealth Editors: *Created Wealthy, See Yourself Wealthy, Infinite Wealth Here and Beyond, It Gives God Pleasure To Give You Wealth, Wealth Is Your Destiny, The ABC's Of Wealth, Laugh Your Way To The Bank, The Richest King Who Ever Lived, and The Divinity of Christ Within You.*

They are Excellent Reading Material for you to Read them to Lisa out loud. We want her to Hear them. That is a part of her Wealth Training. Our goal is for Lisa to both Hear and Feel the Wealth you Read during Story Time. Mary and Jason, we literally want you to <u>Saturate Your Womb (Lisa's Immediate Atmosphere) with Wealth.</u> The classical music as well as the Wealth Tapes can be heard over the intercom twenty-four hours a day, seven days a week. Oh, and with respect to the library, it Houses millions of books that will, without question, Expand Your Wealthy Thinking. It is open any time of the day or night, so please feel free to go there any time you wish. Someone is always on staff to assist you."

On his way out the door, Dr. Lee touched Mary's stomach and said, "Hello, Lisa. This is Dr. Lee. How are you doing today? Are you ready for your Wealth Training? It is going to be awesome. I promise. Let us know what you think!" "Mary and Jason," said Dr. Lee, "the staff is eager to meet you one on one, but they want to give you an extra day or two to get used to your new home. We want you to <u>Soak up this Wealthy Environment like a sponge.</u>

Feel free to go outside, take a walk around the Wealth Center, or call upon your personal chauffeur to drive you anywhere you wish to visit. Your chef, Jeffrey, will also be on hand any time you need him to prepare a meal for you. Or you can whip up something yourself at any time. Enjoy the rest of the day."

Immediately after Dr. Lee left the master suite, the telephone rang. "Hello, may I speak to Mary and Jason please? This is Ty of The Wealth Center. I have you both on speaker phone. I am Dr. Rich's Personal Accountant. Did Lamar talk to you about the $1 Million a year Stipend that you and Mary will be receiving?"

Mary and Jason were so stunned, they could barely speak. "Welllllllll…" Ty said, "Dr. Rich probably also told you that as soon as you selected a name for Lisa, we all agreed to extend to Lisa $5 Million a year, for the rest of her life. That $5 Million does not include all the Wealth Lisa will <u>Most Definitely Attract</u> on her own as a result of this Extensive and Intensive Wealth Training. This Money is just an Incentive for you because you <u>Participated in this Priceless Study</u>!

Mary and Jason, I was just calling to let you know that these Accounts have been opened, Effective Immediately. It is your Account and you can do with it as you will. But please be advised that aside from these Monies, you are also free to go shopping anywhere for anything you wish, any time you wish. Just bring all the receipts to me, and I will take care of the bills personally. We have that kind of agreement with unlimited establishments around the world.

There Is No Limit as to how much Money you can spend. But everything you purchase must Reflect Wealth. That is what The Wealth Center is all about. It is our collective responsibility to <u>Maintain a Wealthy Atmosphere</u> for Lisa at all times, along with her developing simultaneously a Pleasant Attitude. One must possess Wealth as well as a <u>Right Attitude about Wealth!</u>"

Mary and Jason could not believe their ears. A sum total of $6 Million had just been Deposited into their Bank Account. And all they had to do was <u>Participate in Programming</u> Lisa daily with Wealth. Mary would never have to worry about Money again! Godspeed Accounting Services, Mary's favorite Law Firm, which specializes in Accounting and Law, would handle all the paper work and business arrangements necessary to setting up Mary and Jason's Accounts and Lisa's Trust Funds.

Mary was now a Wealthy woman. She said out loud: "I am Wealthy now. You hear that Lisa. We are not going to get Wealthy. We are already Wealthy. Lisa, you my baby girl, will be born Wealthy. And with all this Wealth we infuse you with, you will only get Wealthier, Even In Your Mother's Womb. It is surreal!!!"

"Was this a fairytale?" thought Mary and Jason. This did not seem real. But as Mary and Jason had discovered in their first limo ride to The Wealth Center, Wealth is Real. Anything less is the fairytale. Being in lack, or living from paycheck to paycheck is merely an illusion.

That was the purpose of being at The Wealth Center. Here, in this particular surrounding, Lisa would not be exposed to the fairytales that parents read to their children – fairytales such as Hansel and Gretel, Cinderella, and The Three Little Bears. Lisa would be <u>Exposed to Stories that Promote Wealth, Abundance, Riches, Increase, and Prosperity.</u>

She would be treated to adventures, travel, expeditions, and experiences that encourage one to Appreciate the Wealth Jehovah God Created. And she would be Gifted with the Wisdom to handle herself and all her God-Given Wealth Wisely, while she was yet In Her Mother's Belly. She would still enjoy doing all the things that children her age like to do, but with one exception. She would be open to a world that encourages one to develop thought processes that defy the norm.

The Wealth Center would not keep Lisa inside a bubble (locked into Affluence and Luxury Only), but would also <u>provide her with an Early Childhood Education and/or Human Growth and Development situation that does not fit within the regular confines of traditional education. This whole Wealth Study could be viewed as a Pilot Study for others to emulate!</u>

Chapter Seven

THE CHAPEL SERVICES

The Sabbaticals (Chapel Services) were working! At each Reading During Story Time, Mary could Feel her Lisa kick. Lisa obviously enjoyed Mary and Jason Reading To Her Out Loud. A bond was being formed between father, mother, and daughter, which would be unbreakable.

Lisa's Ears Were Open To Wealth! She could Feel Wealth Surrounding Her In Her Mother's Womb. She could also Feel the Wealth in Mary and Jason's Atmosphere (The Wealth Center). The Wealth Center's Subliminal Programming and Biblical Meditation were working, and Lisa was letting everyone know that she Comprehended their Wealth Strategies. Everyone was pleased!!! Throughout every day and night, the Wealth Tapes never stopped playing.

In The Womb, Lisa had "Visions of Wealth Dancing In Her Head." Lisa Never Got Tired of

Hearing about All The Wealth in God's Universe, and she would have plenty of time to explore her world when she got here via birth.

Lisa heard the message preached over and over in Chapel Services each Sabbath day about the Wealthy Creation God Created, and she was Amazed! Her Love for God, even In Her Mother's Womb, was Phenomenal and Unprecedented. No one would know just how much!!!

But that Phenomenon is exactly why Evangelist Pearl Price was hired by The Wealth Center – to provide an Interpretation of God that most clergy and lay men and lay women often overlook.

One might find this hard to believe, but it could be easy for any average church-going member to conclude that God is abusive or broke, after listening to the same sermon on sin week after week after week. For some reason or another, some pastors portray God as a mean Father who is sitting on his throne just waiting to beat every sinner over the head with a stick if they get out of line, out of character, or out of the Will of God. That is not a practical or wise thing to do if anyone had less than a perfect father or dad who absolutely could never compare to God!

God is a Loving Father who Cares so much for his children (us) until He would allow His Son, Jesus Christ, to die on the cross for our sins. "For God so loved the world, that He gave His only Begotten Son, that whosoever believeth in Him, should not perish, but have everlasting life" (John 3:16). God wants to have a <u>Healthy Relationship</u> with each and every person, regardless of anyone's race, creed, ethnic background, socio-economic status, or church affiliation.

Other pastors are very adamant about preaching on the Scripture, "The love of money is the root of all evil" (1 Timothy 6:10), while on the other hand, impressing upon everyone what will happen if he or she does not pay tithes regularly: "Will a man rob God? Yet, ye have robbed me. But ye say, Wherein have we robbed thee? In tithes and offerings. Ye are cursed with a curse: for ye have robbed me, even this whole nation. Bring ye all the tithes into the storehouse, that there may be meat in mine house, and prove me now herewith, saith the Lord of Hosts, if I will not open you the windows of heaven, and pour you out a blessing, that there shall not be room enough to receive it. And I will rebuke the devourer for your sakes, and he shall not destroy the fruits of your ground; neither shall your vine cast her fruit before the time in the field, saith the Lord of Hosts. And all nations shall call you Blessed: for ye shall be a delightsome land, saith the Lord of Hosts" (Malachi 3:8-12).

In Mary and Jason's case, they had faithfully paid their tithes and offerings on a regular basis for years, yet they had struggled financially. No one, in either Lake Geneva, Wisconsin or Kennebunkport, Maine had taken the time to Program Mary and Jason's mind so they could see how Abundant God Actually Is!!! It was just assumed that they should automatically know how to be Successful. After all, everyone else seemed to instinctively know what to do. Only The Wealth Center had thought enough of Mary and Jason to approach them with an Opportunity of a Lifetime. And Mary and Jason were smart enough to capitalize on the moment!!!

What would their life be like if they had not been hand selected to be a part of the Wealth Study? They would still be listening to those same drab messages every week that would keep them on the outside looking in. They would be forever bound by negative financial circumstances. The Wealth Center was only teaching the Gospel that the Lord commissioned everyone to tell.

Jesus said these words in Luke 4:18-19 concerning himself: "The Spirit of the Lord is upon me, because he hath anointed me to preach the Gospel to the poor, he hath sent me to heal the brokenhearted, to preach deliverance to the captives, and recovering of sight to the blind, to set at liberty them that are bruised, to preach the acceptable year of the Lord."

Unfortunately in verses 28 and 29 of that same Passage of Scripture, it reads, "And all they in the synagogue, when they heard these things, were filled with wrath, and rose up, and thrust him out of the city, and led him unto the brow of the hill whereon their city was built, that they might cast him down headlong."

If God was not concerned about Wealth, why would Jesus go out of his way to "preach the Gospel to the poor?" The church would argue this one Scripture to the death: "The poor always ye have with you…" (John 12:8). That statement does not mean what most clergy think it means. We will always have the poor with us because not everyone who is poor will accept the Gospel as the Gospel Truth. If every poor person who heard the Gospel would believe the Gospel, poverty would no longer exist.

There are people who still believe that having lots of money is a sin. And unfortunately, most of the people who have that kind of mentality are in the church world. At The Wealth Center, Mary and Jason were taught to accept as True that poverty is sin, and that everything else is only an illusion. How did they come to this conclusion? God's Creation – the Universe, the world, and the Garden of Eden was full of Supernatural Wealth. If you go to the furthest east and travel as far west as you can go, You Cannot Even Fathom All The Wealth!!! If you travel to the deepest south and end up in the deepest north, you still would not be able to put a price tag on God!

On the same token, if you took a sheet of paper, 8 ½ by 11, and wrote the number 9 from the left edge of the paper to the far right edge as small as you could, then you went back and added in all the commas in the prospective places, and then added the number 1 to such a number, which in this case, the whole equation equals a sum of money, how much money would you actually have? The wisest mathematician or economist probably could not adequately Determine The Definite Amount Of Money.

That is how Wealthy everyone is, yet, Satan has done a great job in undermining that Wealth. As a result, most people buy into the notion that having Money is a taboo. Satan may be a father of lies, but that does not mean that he does not know the Real Truth about Money. He just wants to keep that Knowledge of Wealth a Secret so you cannot see the Love Of God.

The average person will say, "Just as long as I have Money to pay my bills and food on my table, I am content." Fortunately, that may be their personal way of thinking, but God wants to give them so much Money they would have enough Money Left Over To Enjoy _and_ to Share with those who do not have it. A person might say, "I do not need $1 Million, but if you had that Amount of Money, you would at least have enough Money to buy somebody a cup of coffee or a sausage biscuit. A broke person would not be in such a position to provide for himself or herself, let alone help anyone else.

Only a stingy person, like the Rich Young Ruler in Luke 18:18-27 would not want to Share The Wealth. He, the Rich, Young Ruler, "went away sorrowful because he had great possessions" that he wanted to keep for himself. Notice that Jesus did not condemn that Ruler because he had Money, which would have been the case if God wanted his children to walk around "broke, busted, and disgusted." Rather, when Jesus said to this man, "Go and sell what you have and give to the poor," he meant that the man had enough Wealth to be a Blessing to someone in need. You cannot put Money into anyone's hands if you do not have it.

Here at The Wealth Center, it was the personal belief of everyone on staff that "Man shall not live by bread alone, but by every word that proceedeth out of the mouth of God" (Matthew 4:4). In other words, it is not a good idea to only preach on certain scriptures, while overlooking others.

If you are going to preach on Malachi 3:10 (tithes and offerings), then why not quote the scripture in 3 John 1: 2, which says, "Beloved, I wish above all things that thou mayest Prosper and be in Health, even as thy Soul Prospers?" Or why not preach on the Scripture, "...Whatever he doeth shall Prosper" (Psalms 1:3)? Or why not preach on the Scripture, "But thou broughtest us out into a Wealthy Place" (Psalms 66:12)? If God did not care about Wealth, why would he bother bringing anyone into a Wealthy Place?

After all, Timothy did write in 2 Timothy 3:16-17: "All scripture [From Genesis 1:1 to Revelation 22:21] is given by Inspiration of God, and is Profitable for doctrine, for reproof, for correction, for instruction in righteousness, that the man of God may be perfect, thoroughly furnished unto all good works." If the entire Bible is the Inspired Word of God, we absolutely cannot deny the Power of God to bring anyone into Wealth. In Deuteronomy 8:18, it is written: "But thou shalt remember the Lord thy God; for it is He that giveth thee Power to get Wealth, that he may Establish His Covenant which He Sware unto they fathers, as it is this day."

Evangelist Pearl Price had been unlike any of the other candidates who had applied for a position at The Wealth Center as an Anointed Chaplain. She understood better than most the True Nature and Character of God, and his Real Intent towards His People. Yes, "God does have People!!!" The other applicants had formal degrees in Theology, which is not a bad thing if you have a Correct Image of God, yet they like the religious sect of Jesus' day, had somehow missed God. They had gotten so caught up in Adam and Eve's sin, and how Satan had deceived the woman in the Garden of Eden, until they failed to see exactly why Satan went out of his way to mislead them.

The applicants refused to elaborate on the fact that Adam and Eve were Created Astronomically and Infinitely Wealthy!!! Everything they needed to live and survive had been Created by God before they came on the scene. Adam and Eve were living in a Debt-Free Economy. They had Plenty of food and drink. They had Superb Living Conditions. They had Permanent Employment. They were Infinitely Healthy. In that Perfect Arrangement, Jesus Christ was the Head of their Government. And that was the way God intended it to be. Anywhere and everywhere they both looked, Riches, Wealth, Abundance, Prosperity, Increase, and Fruitfulness Abounded.

That is why Satan came – to cheat Adam and Eve – the First Family - out of their Supernatural Inheritance and God-Ordained Birthright – a Birthright of Infinite Wealth. If he could get <u>the first man</u> <u>(the first God-Man)</u> and <u>the first woman</u> <u>(The First Woman Of God</u> (God's Woman First) (husband and wife team) to doubt God's True Nature and Character, mankind as God Created it would be lost forever. Or so Satan thought. <u>God would have the Last Word, and it would be Good!!!</u> Thus, The Wealth Center, which Had Always Existed with God from the very beginning, would be Established by God to Reinstitute one's faith in God and His Perfect Creation.

Chaplain Price was <u>the very Epitome of God's Nature</u>. She had been named Pearl by her mom and dad, both of whom held a Doctorate in Divinity, so that she would always be reminded that she was a "<u>Pearl of Great Price</u>" as mentioned in the Gospel of Matthew (Matthew 13: 46). Evangelist Pearl Price, when it came to seeing the Light, had literally taken the words from Colossians 1:13: "translated into the kingdom of his dear Son" to a place no one else had dared to go: all the way back to the Garden of Eden, to Spiritually See, Feel, Hear, and Know what God had intended for the rest of us to be translated into His Kingdom.

No one would ever dream of coming into something, and not taking the time to know what he or she was actually coming into. No athlete in his right mind would try out to be a quarterback for any football team without first knowing something about the team in which he wanted to join. In the business world, any person applying for a Corporate Executive Officer position with a major firm would not think of going into an interview without taking the time to do research on the company.

On the same token, why would anyone want to enter the Kingdom of God and not know something about the Kingdom or the King? Why would anyone want to work for the United Nations and not know what the United Nations' employees do? Why would anyone want to be crowned Miss America, Miss Universe, or Miss World and not want to represent their constituents in the best possible manner? How could anyone be a Child of the Most High God, and not strive to Ascribe to the Highest Standard Imaginable?

Many individuals would undoubtedly frown upon The Wealth Center's Endeavors to Facilitate Wealth, especially if they viewed Having Wealth as an atrocity. They might even go out on a limb and label The Wealth Center as some type of spiritual monster, or false prophecy ministry that needed to be alleviated.

But perhaps it is easier to take the lesser road and convince the world that we have nothing better to do than complain about what is not working. Perhaps it is better if we all sit around and cry into our cup of tea while we discuss the 25 Zillion reasons why our economy is spiraling deeper and deeper into a financial deficit. Perhaps it is easier to blame our high unemployment rate on the Democratic, Republican, or Independent Party. Or perhaps it is easier to blame our misfortunes on racism, sexism, ageism, prejudice, bias, bigotry, narrow-mindedness, and negative predispositions. <u>Is it not plausible to think of ourselves as Spiritually Living In God's Economy where only Wealth Exists?</u>

What if Nicodemus in John 3:4 was ahead of his time when he asked Jesus this question: "How can a man be born when he is old? Can he enter the second time into his mother's womb, and be born"? Perhaps Jesus' statement: "You must be born again" (Verse 3) threw all the Theologians off in a Dramatically Spiritual way. Perhaps this Short Novel, The Wealth Center, was merely an instrument to demonstrate to the world the Possibility of taking Creation to the Highest Dimension by teaching Willing Participants how to exercise his or her own Creative Power to its FULLEST capacity.

John the Baptist Rejoiced In His Mother's Womb, and was filled with the Holy Ghost when he heard the Salutation of Mary, the Mother of Jesus. We can all get caught up in Genetics, Genetic Makeup, and DNA, but has anyone forgotten the Genetic Makeup of God? If we are Created in the Image of God according to the Book of Genesis (Genesis 1:26-27), would that not mean that deep inside of us, we have Jehovah God's Genetic Makeup inside of us? <u>*Would that not mean that we could take what we have been Endowed With And Expand It Exponentially?*</u>

Why would it be so hard for an entire world to Believe that we are Financially Endowed with the very Image and Essence of Almighty God, and that we were born with that Image already intact? True, not everyone was born with a silver spoon in his or her mouth, technically or literally, as we would define it. After all, we, as humans, are not qualified to even second guess God's actual viewpoint on who is or is not <u>Born Wealthy.</u>

Spiritually, we all were, in fact, Born Wealthy because we were literally Born Into The Wealthy World that Jehovah God, our Heavenly Father Created. It was He who actually Conceived us In The Womb so that we could be Born Into An Infinitely Wealthy World. It was his idea for us to Behold All The Wealth that He Created so that we could Expose All That Wealth to others who were blind to all the Wealth that is Around All Of Us!!!

As soon as an infant is old enough to take his first step, he or she begins the process of exploring everything in his or her environment. That is why he or she will spend countless hours touching everything in sight. They are curious about the things around them. Unfortunately, some adults lose that Anointing of "Wonder." The Wonder Years should never have an expiration date for anyone. Every day is a Wonder!!!

Wealth is Available in Large, Massive Quantities to everyone Equally, yet, very few individuals will Take The Time To discover That Wealth. Few individuals will try to <u>Step Outside The Box</u> of limitation and lack to even endeavor to Develop A Wealthy Imagination – the kind of Imagination where Any Good Thing And Every Good Thing is possible.

Those same individuals will somehow manage to convince the rest of us that it is wrong to think about having Millions, Billions, Trillions, and Zillions of Dollars, Expensive Cars, Huge Mansions, or Massive Bank Accounts, let alone Possess Them.

On the other hand, most individuals would spend a lot of wasted time and motion arguing about the Wealthiest of the Wealthy and how much of a tax break they should or should not get. It is assumed that those with the Most Money should carry everyone else's tax burden.

At The Wealth Center, it is a common practice to teach selected participants the Uncommon Wealth Principle of Appreciating Wealth to the Highest Degree. In short, you can never have what you do not wish for others to have. If you envy others' Wealth Status, you will either never Have Wealth, or you will have limited Wealth, and not Infinite Wealth. If you believe that Having Wealth is wrong, you sabotage your own Opportunity To Become Wealthy.

For that reason alone, every participant in The Wealth Study is not only taught Wealth Principles that will Enhance his or her Wealth, he or she is also taught how to protect themselves from the physical, mental, emotional, social, financial, and academic thieves and robbers who might try to decrease such a High Self-Worth.

At some point in your life, you just have to learn not to listen to the naysayers, doomsayers, critics, and enemies of Wealth who will tell you 25 Zillion reasons why you cannot be Wealthy, but will refuse to listen to your <u>one reason why you can be</u>. Here at The Chapel Services, everyone understood that Having Wealth was God-Ordained and <u>a normal part of life, not to mention NATURAL!!!</u>

Chapter Eight

THE AWAKENING

Dr. Lee wanted to ensure that Lisa would be given the Best State Of The Art Prenatal Wealth Care Available, therefore, he scheduled a private interview session with only Mary, himself, and the psychologist on call, Dr. Gabriel Wells.

During a private session with Jason earlier, they had discovered Mary's difficulty in finding employment. They understood Lisa's desires to be a Senator, attorney, etcetera, but she had fallen short of her goals due to a lack of High Self-Worth and Self-Esteem. Their Objective was to bring Mary on board by Adding Value to her Self-Image.

In essence, they would be Creating a new, emotional Self-Portrait of Mary so she could see how Worthy she was. Without it, she could unconsciously undermine and sabotage Lisa's Wealthy Programming. This session would allow

Mary to Heal Emotionally, Mentally, Physically, Financially, Academically, and Spiritually.

Mary would be debriefed and de-programmed of her former failures by all the Wealth Programming Techniques AND Biblical Meditation Strategies utilized by The Wealth Center to the point where she would feel complete, none of which had anything to do with the $6 Million that had been deposited into their account. It was important that Mary felt phenomenally successful in every respect. Otherwise, the Wealth Study would be pointless.

After Mary experienced the necessary emotional closure and Healing, she would have a new lease on life. Additionally, on another day and time, both Jason and The Wealth Center staff would surprise Mary with a wedding that she wanted – a wedding with all the trimmings – an Expensive wedding gown, an Expensive reception, a Perfect honeymoon in Hawaii, and a Great vacation home to come home to. She would come to her own wedding in a white stretch limo. Mary and Jason had had a simple wedding because of a lack of funds, but this time around, the groom would marry her in Style and Class just as the bride had wanted.

With respect to personality, Jason was comfortable expressing his ideas on canvas, whereas Mary was the writer in the family. Writing about her own new life would allow her to <u>Heal Quickly</u> so she could <u>Attract Greater Happiness and Wealth</u>. Mary's new life would be <u>Greater</u>

than what she thought she had lost out on. Mary, through Giving Birth to Lisa, would get her life back, just new and improved.

That was why Dr. Wells was on hand. Mary needed to release all her emotions in a safe place. And Mary did release. She cried uncontrollably among friends. She was a new woman with a New-Found Identity and Purpose – Enjoying every second of her life on earth, knowing <u>She Mattered</u> and was Important to God and to the Universe!

Learning how to Feel Wealthy had gotten Mary to this moment in her life where she was aware of herself. Her Dreams would be realized. She was a Great Thinker and a Great Planner. <u>She had Great Ideas</u> that could make the Entire Universe A Better Place – all because she had Discovered her own Worthiness. No one can put a price on his or her own High Self-worth. <u>It is Absolutely Invaluable and priceless!!!</u>

When Mary left the meeting with Dr. Lee and Dr. Wells, she went to find her husband, Jason. Jason knew the instant change in his beloved wife who was the <u>Love of his Life.</u> He knew she had experienced an encounter of some kind, but he did not know what. Instead of asking Mary questions about what had happened, he embraced the moment. He got his release.

Jason loved Mary with all the fiber of his being. It had been he who had sped up their wedding because he wanted to spend the rest of his life with her. He could not wait to be with her! He had wanted to get married when Mary had wanted to wait.

He knew Mary was having difficulty in finding herself, but he would not let a lack of Money come between them. Jason was bringing in enough Money from his Commissions at the art gallery to Sustain them for a while, but he only had enough Money for the most basic of weddings. Perhaps he should have waited for the both of them to be Financially Stable before Marriage, like Mary and their friends and family had suggested. Perhaps they all had been right about a lot of things.

His desire to spend the rest of his life with Mary had put Mary under such financial strain, she collapsed in the employment office. But, then again, that is what got them to The Wealth Center in the first place. If Mary had not gone to the employment office on the day she did, Jason was absolutely certain that they would have never met Dr. Lee, their OB-GYN, or Dr. Rich. They most definitely would not be here at The Wealth Center.

Jason would make it up to Mary somehow. *He would spend the rest of his life making everything up to her. She was his baby girl – his one true love – his only love. And he would spend the rest of his life making his wife very, very happy!!!!!!*

And he would start by programming his own mind with all the Wealth Tapes Available to them. *He would make sure his wife had everything she needed. She would never have to worry about anything again – ever!!!*

Chapter Nine

THE FIRST BIBLE STUDY

Jason decided to go into The Wealth Center's Library (Wealthy Mindset) on those days when Mary was being Pampered at The Wealth Center Spa. Jason would go to the Library and Browse through all the Reading Materials. There must have been a Trillion Books at his finger tips. He would <u>spend hours at a time Programming his Subconscious Mind With Wealth.</u>

He wanted his wife and daughter to have all the Advantages In Life, and he wanted them to be Programmed with all the Wealth The Wealth Center would provide. But, as a man, and as the head of his house, he Felt he should take the lead in helping Mary and his unborn daughter, Lisa, Discover That Wealth. He would step up to the plate and do some Wealth Programming of his own. Who knows? Perhaps he could encourage all his male friends to take the time to Program themselves to <u>Receive Astronomical Wealth.</u> No family should have to struggle financially. But first, Jason would take care of his household first. He would begin at the Wealth Center Chapel.

Jason took Mary and his unborn daughter, Lisa, into the chapel where they could have some privacy, and he began to conduct his very first Bible Study. This was the first time in his life that <u>he had actually led a family devotional</u>, as he called it. But it would most definitely not be the last time he would lead his family – his immediate family – into such an intimate moment. *As far as Jason was concerned, any man who loved God half as much as he say he did would not settle for anything less than leading his wife and children into daily WORSHIP!!! After all, God did say in Psalms 113:3: "From the rising of the sun unto the going down of the same, the Lord's name is to be praised."*

He began Reading the King James Version of the Bible, starting at 1Kings 10:1:

"And when the Queen of Sheba heard of the fame of Solomon concerning the Name of the Lord, she came to prove him with hard questions. And she came to Jerusalem with A Very Great Train, with camels that bare spices, and Very Much Gold, and Precious Stones: and when she was come to Solomon, she communed with him of all that was in her heart. And Solomon told her all her questions: there was not anything hid from the King, which he told her not. And when the Queen of Sheba had seen all Solomon's Wisdom, and the House That He Had Built, and the meat of his table, and the sitting of his servants, and the attendance of his ministers, and their apparel, and his cupbearers, and his ascent by which he went up into the House of the Lord; there was no more Spirit in her.

And she said to the King, It was a true report that I heard in mine own land of thy Acts and of thy Wisdom. Howbeit I believed not the words, until I came, and mine eyes had seen it: and behold, <u>the half was not told me</u>: thy Wisdom and Prosperity <u>exceedeth</u> the fame which I heard. <u>Happy are thy men</u>, <u>happy are these thy servants</u>, which stand continually before thee, and that hear thy Wisdom. Blessed be the Lord thy God, which delighted in thee, to set thee on the throne of Israel: because the Lord loved Israel forever, therefore made He thee King, to do judgment and justice.

And she gave the King an hundred and Twenty Talents of Gold, and of spices Very Great Store, and Precious Stones: there came no more such Abundance of Spices as these which the Queen of Sheba gave to King Solomon. And the navy also of Hiram, that brought Gold from Ophir, brought in from Ophir great plenty of almug trees, and precious stones. And the King made of the almug trees pillars for the House of the Lord, and for the King's house, harps also and psalteries for singers: there came no such almug trees, nor were seen unto this day.

<u>And King Solomon gave unto the queen of Sheba all her desire, whatsoever she asked,</u> beside that which Solomon gave her of his Royal Bounty. So she turned and went to her own country, she and her servants. Now the Weight of Gold that came to Solomon In One Year was Six Hundred Threescore And Six Talents Of Gold. Beside that he had of the merchantmen, and of the traffick of the spice merchants, and of all the Kings of Arabia, and of the Governors of the country.

And King Solomon made two hundred targets of beaten Gold: six hundred shekels of Gold went to one target. And he made three hundred shekels of beaten Gold; three pounds of Gold went to one shield: and the King put them in the house of the forest of Lebanon. Moreover the King made a great throne of ivory, and overlaid it with the Best Gold. The throne had six steps, and the top of the throne was round behind: and there were stays on either side on the place of the seat, and two lions stood beside the stays.

And twelve lions stood there on the one side and on the other upon the six steps: there was not the like made in any Kingdom. And all king Solomon's drinking vessels were of Gold, and all the vessels of the house of the forest of Lebanon were of pure Gold; none were of Silver: it was nothing accounted of in the days of Solomon. For the King had at sea a navy of Tharshish with the navy of Hiram: once in three year came the navy of Tharshish, bringing Gold, and Silver, ivory, and apes, and peacocks. So King Solomon exceeded all the Kings of the earth for Riches and for wisdom. And all the earth sought to Solomon, to hear his wisdom, which God had put in his heart. And they brought every man his present, vessels of Silver, and vessels of Gold, and garments, and armour, and spices, horses and mules, a rate year by year. And Solomon gathered together chariots and horsemen: and he had a thousand and four hundred chariots, and twelve thousand horsemen, whom he bestowed in the cities for chariots, and with the King at Jerusalem.

And the King made silver to be in Jerusalem as stones, and cedars made he to be as the sycamore trees that are in the vale, for Abundance. And Solomon had horses brought out of Egypt, and linen yard: the King's merchants received the linen yard at price. And a chariot came up and went out of Egypt for six hundred shekels of Silver, and an horse for an hundred and fifty: and so for all the Kings of the Hittites, and for the Kings of Syria, did they bring them out by their means."

Jason said, "Lisa, did you enjoy that Bible reading? King Solomon was the Richest King who ever lived and I wanted you to know that you, too, can live as well as he. Did you notice that King Solomon drank out of gold cups? So shall you!!! And I am here to tell you that you should never settle for anything less than that!!!

You are a Princess. You are a Queen. You are destined for Greatness, and you were Set Apart To Show Forth That Wealth to the world.

Your mom and I will continue to remind you who you are by <u>Reading this Passage of Scripture and other Bible Scriptures daily.</u>

According to the Bible in Joshua 1:8, it says: "But, this book of the law shall not depart out of thy mouth. <u>But thou</u> <u>shalt meditate therein day and night</u>, that thou mayest observe to do according to all that is written therein: for then thou shalt make thy way Prosperous, and then <u>thou shalt have Good Success</u>." Also, Lisa in the Book of Psalms Chapter 1, verses 1-3, it says, "Blessed is the man that walketh not in the counsel of the ungodly, nor standeth in the way of sinners, nor sitteth in the seat of the scornful. But <u>his delight is in the law of the Lord</u>, and <u>in his law doth he meditate day and night</u>. And he shall be like a tree planted by the rivers of water, that bringeth forth his Fruit in his season; his leaf also shall not wither, and whatsoever he doeth shall Prosper."

"One more passage of Scripture to read Lisa, and we will be done. But I promise that I will read this one to you every night. It is your mom's favorite Scripture, and it is taken from Deuteronomy 28:1-14. Listen carefully to what it says:

"And it shall come to pass, if thou shalt hearken diligently unto the voice of the Lord thy God, to observe and to do all his commandments which I command thee this day, that the Lord thy God will set thee on high above all nations of the earth: And all these blessings shall come on thee, and overtake thee, if thou shalt hearken unto the

voice of the Lord thy God. Blessed shalt thou
be in the city, and blessed shalt thou be in the
field. Blessed shall be the fruit of thy body, and
the fruit of thy ground, and the fruit of thy cattle,
the increase of thy kine, and flocks of thy sheep.
Blessed shall be thy basket and thy store. Blessed
shalt thou be when thou comest in, and blessed
shalt thou be when thou goest out. The Lord shall
cause thine enemies that rise up against thee to
be smitten before thy face: they shall come out
against thee one way and flee before thee seven
ways. The Lord shall command the blessing
upon thee in thy storehouses, and in all that thou
settest thine hand unto; and he shall bless thee
in the land which the Lord thy God giveth thee.
The Lord shall establish thee an holy people unto
himself, as he hath sworn unto thee, if thou shalt
keep the commandments of the Lord thy God, and
walk in his ways. And all people of rhe earth shall
see that thou art called by the name of the Lord;
and they shall be afraid of thee. And the Lord
shall make thee plenteous in goods, in the fruit
of thy body, and in the fruit of thy cattle, and in
the fruit of thy ground, in the land which <u>the Lord
sware unto thy fathers</u> to give thee. The Lord shall
open unto thee his good treasure, the heaven to
give the rain unto thy land in his season, and to
bless all work of thine hand: and thou shalt lend
unto many nations, and thou shalt not borrow.
And the Lord shall make thee the head, and not
the tail; and thou shalt be above only, and thou
shalt not be beneath; if that thou hearken unto
the commandments of the Lord thy God, which
I command thee this day, to observe and to do

them. And thou shalt not go aside from any of the words which I command thee this day, to the right hand, or to the left, to go after other gods to serve them."

"Lisa, did you like that? Always remember, Lisa, the importance of Meditating In God's Word (The Bible) daily. In doing this, you will become what you Meditate in, Read, And Look at daily. That is the Beauty of Meditation!!!

We all are Programming you to <u>Look At Wealth</u> daily so you can become that Wealth. As you become that Wealth, you can Impart that Same Wealth Strategy to others. The world is waiting. So, Absorb All This Wealth Training like a sponge!!! You understand, Lisa?" At that moment, the baby kicked. Lisa understood!!!

Chapter Ten

THE LAMAZE ROOM

Mary was now coming to the end of the trimester, and she was starting to look like a new mom. She was glowing. She Looked Radiant, and Felt Beautiful, even more so after this morning's Lamaze Class. As Jason had helped her with her breathing, Mary's mind traveled ahead to the day of her Delivery. She Was Looking Forward to bringing Lisa into the world. But, she was Feeling something else as well.

With each breath she took in the Lamaze Class, she became more aware of her own body and the body of her Unborn Child. She did not know why, but she could not wait to Read A New Story About Wealth to Lisa every day. She could almost Feel All The Wealth Available from the Garden of Eden up to now, flowing directly to her daughter each time she Read to her. Mary thought that was due to the Environment of the Lamaze

Class. Obviously, The Wealth Center knew what they were doing when they designed this State Of The Art Lamaze Classroom!!!

Jason was the artist in the family, yet, it was Mary who Most Appreciated The Environment, The Atmosphere and the Peaceful Surroundings of The Wealth Center. Mary had been brought up in the church, and it was customary for her family to go to church every Saturday at 6:00 a.m. to <u>Pray and Meditate</u>. They believed the 7th day of the week, and not the 1st day of the week, was the day God personally set aside for Spiritual Worship. Of course, everyone had a right to practice his or her own Faith in the way he or she chose. During those Saturday morning services, everyone sat quietly in his or her pew and enjoyed the silence, which meant everything to Mary because she was <u>Most Creative</u> during those peaceful moments.

Here in the Lamaze Room, as Mary called it, there was a Peacefulness that she deeply longed for. The walls had been painted forest green, and <u>the serene aura it gave was profound!</u> Mary felt so safe in this room, she could easily slip into a Deep Relaxation that the greatest massage therapist would die for. Mary could just close her eyes and mentally go anywhere she wanted to go.

Also, there were full-length mirrors which traveled alongside all walls of the room. Mary loved to look at herself in mirrors as she passed them, and this room was no exception. This was the one room in The Wealth Center where Mary could check out her "<u>femininity</u>" or <u>feminine side to gauge her maternity look</u>. In the beginning of her pregnancy, it had been Jason who was the most excited about having a child. But, now, Mary realized that she was about to give birth to her first child, and reality was starting to set in.

This was a lot to take in. Mary was a mom now, though not technically until after the childbirth, and Dr. Lee had exercised a lot of patience in talking to them about Prenatal matters. Mary never thought she would be here at the Wealth Center thinking about things such as Breast Feeding, First, Second or Third Trimesters, Natural Childbirth, Parent Education Classes, Childbirth Classes, The Bradley Method, Lamaze Classes, or any other Kind of Classes.

Nor had Mary thought about her Delivery Date on Friday, October 13th. When Mary was a child, she had overheard a conversation about a woman getting raped and becoming pregnant as a result. Mary was only four years old when she heard this tidbit of information, yet, it had left her permanently scarred with lots of fears and phobias.

She associated the rape and pregnancy with insufferable, intolerable, and unbearable pain. Therefore, this fear led to Mary not wanting to have sexual intercourse with any man. For that reason, she was most emphatic about not having children. In fact, Mary avoided all conversations about such matters altogether. It is a miracle that Mary was pregnant. She had vowed never to have children. She was not looking forward to the pain of Childbirth many women talked about.

Thankfully, the Lamaze Instructor's Personal Assistant and Coach, Samuel, knew what to do when Mary came to Lamaze Class. He knew how to get Mary to Relax. But, first, she would have to look at the very thing that caused her to have panic attacks.

Here at The Wealth Center, every Principle that was taught to each participant was based on Spiritual and Biblical Scriptures. According to the verse in 1 John 4:18: "There is no fear in love; but Perfect Love casteth out fear; because fear hath torment. He that feareth is not made Perfect In Love."

Mary was afraid, and that fear was tormenting her more than she knew, and Samuel was here to help. He would get Mary started in her Prenatal Care Techniques right away! Part of that Prenatal Care involved Mary dissolving her fear of pain during Childbirth. Otherwise, that fear could very well be passed on to Lisa. Samuel was not about to let that happen!

First, Samuel took lots of pictures of The Birthing Room to make Mary feel at ease. It was obvious that Mary had a passion for interior decorating. She was into the décor and the special layout of every room of The Wealth Center, and she had delightfully redecorated many of the rooms. Therefore, Mary would enjoy getting a personal feel for the Environment she would

Give Birth In when that <u>Special Moment came for Lisa to make her Grand Debut into the world.</u>

Samuel knew that Mary also loved water and the ocean. Mary and Jason had visited SeaWorld in Orlando, Florida several times. That was the one thing Mary and Jason <u>Could Afford</u>. Samuel, on the other hand could not afford to pass up the opportunity to let Mary know that The Birthing Room's predominant colors were ocean blue. This was the one color that was powerful enough to override Mary's fear of Delivery.

Mary had always lived near some form of water. In fact, she and Jason had first met on the beach as Mary sat on the shore staring deeply at the ocean, sipping on ginger ale and munching on an assortment of cheese. Mary had gotten so lost in her own thoughts she had not noticed that Jason was only a few feet away from her, capturing the essence of her beauty on canvas. If the ocean could have that much effect on Mary then, it would most definitely work during Lisa's Delivery!

Samuel had been right!!! Mary Automatically Relaxed and became Tranquil when he showed her the pictures of <u>The Birthing Room</u>. It only took a moment for Mary to Absorb the familiarity of the room and embed those images into her mind. That was Mary's Wealthy Image at its finest hour. Mary was seeing <u>The Birthing Room</u> as a comfortable, exotic, and intimate resort where her possibilities were Infinite. <u>The Birthing Room</u> was not a place of pain, or a source of pain. It was Mary's Wealthy

Place – a safe haven – a place of refuge – and a place of unending joy and total fulfillment. <u>Perfect Love</u> had cast out Mary's fear.

Next, Samuel Read Mary the Bible Scripture taken from Genesis 4:1 Millions of times at one sitting so she could get them into her Spirit and Psyche! The words were as follows: "And Adam knew Eve his wife, and she conceived, and bare Cain, and said, I have gotten a man from the Lord." He would end by saying, "And Jason knew Mary his wife, and Mary conceived and bare Lisa, and said, I have gotten a daughter from the Lord. And her name shall be called Lisa and she shall be Great."

Again, Samuel's strategy worked. Mary began to focus exclusively on the words "Conceived" and "Bare." Every second of the day, Mary kept on seeing herself in her mind's eye Conceiving and Giving Birth to Lisa. In addition, Samuel made sure that Mary focused on the Scripture found in Revelation, "And I shall not be hurt of the second death." This meant that childbirth would not hurt, as she thought it would. Samuel just kept saying over and over every session, "Mary, it is not going to hurt!!! I promise!!!"

In addition to these Meditation and Creative Visualization Tapes, Samuel encouraged Jason to rub Mary's back each time they all watched Childbirth Videos repeatedly on a regular basis. The back rubs kept Mary calm and centered. These Techniques worked like a charm!!! Mary started feeling less apprehensive about her

Delivery. She could not wait for Friday, October 13th to arrive!!!

After Lamaze Class, Mary and Jason had a meeting with the nutritionist, Becky Newhart. It was very important that Mary eat Healthy. With each bite of food, Mary felt more and more confident in teaching Lisa the basics of Health as well as Wealth. Mary wanted Lisa to be <u>Healthy and Wealthy</u>.

Mary requested that The Wealth Center include in its daily regimen an opportunity for Lisa to listen to Health Tapes as well. Dr. Lee, Dr. Rich, and Dr. Wells were pleased with Mary's latest confidence in taking charge of her daughter's Programming. She was taking her planning skills to a level that only she could take it, and they were in awe. This place was doing wonders for Mary, Jason, and Lisa.

The Library staff bought Mary and Jason the latest books on Health for Mary's review. She also asked the nutritionist to send her several copies, if not more, of recipe books that Promoted Health. Mary was delighted to Read the recipes out loud to Jason and Lisa. They would both be Healthy and Wealthy in Mind, Body, Soul, and Spirit. What a Great Gift!!! Mary was really feeling like a wife and mother!!!

Chapter Eleven

LISA'S FIRST PLACE

As Jason was sleeping, Mary went to the nursery that they had lovingly and proudly decorated upon their arrival at The Wealth Center. Everyone can remember buying their first car, their first prom dress, or their first home. Lisa was to be arriving pretty soon, and it was Quintessential for Lisa's First Dwelling Place to be her First Wealthy Place as set forth in Psalms 66:12: "God broughtest us out into a Wealthy Place." <u>Lisa's First Abode had to look absolutely amazing and outstanding</u>!!!

When Lisa was older, she would be shown pictures of how her First Place was craftily designed. She would learn one important lesson about Biblical Economics: In God's Economy, there is no lack or limitation to be found any place. Just as Adam and Eve had everything they needed in the Garden of Eden to live, before they were created by God, everyone at The Wealth Center wanted Lisa to know that no matter where she lived, <u>she would always have more than enough</u>, which is what Wealth is!!!

Unlike Mary and Jason who lived in a Wealthy Environment, without possessing that Material Wealth physically, as had their peers and family, Lisa would never have to live from paycheck to paycheck. She would never live from hand to mouth as most people do. She would never step foot inside any church to hear any member of the clergy say, "God is trying to teach you a lesson. That is why you are broke. What does not kill you will only make you stronger."

The only lesson that God is trying to teach you is how Infinitely Worthy and Wealthy you are <u>right now</u> – not next week, not next month, not next year, not even tomorrow. <u>You are Wealthy NOW</u> and it all begins with a Wealthy Mindset – which was the Purpose of The Wealth Center's Existence – to gladly provide that Wealthy Mentality. "You are not going to get Wealthy. You are already Wealthy." Mary thought! And Lisa's First Place would reek of all that Wealth, with no apologies for being so.

She and her husband, Jason, had picked out every piece of furniture and everything that Lisa needed for her arrival. The walls had been decorated just for Lisa. The walls had been painted emerald green with an ultra gold border at the top and bottom. The Aura of the Room was to give off the Illusion of Wealth. Lisa would always see green and gold. Mary absolutely adored the rich, brown crib they picked out at one of the most Expensive department stores in the country.

Mary loved looking at herself in mirrors, and she deemed it appropriate to have an unbreakable mirror attached to the crib so Lisa would see herself as well. An unbreakable mirror had nothing to do with the superstition that you would have seven years of bad luck if you broke a mirror. She did not want Lisa to hurt herself on any fragments of broken glass. She wanted Lisa to fall in love with herself each time she looked at herself in the mirror. One might think that Mary and Jason were employing this Technique to teach their Lisa how to be vain. This was emphatically not the case! They were teaching their baby girl *the power of loving herself correctly so that she could attract people into her life, especially her future husband, who would love her equally as well as Jehovah God himself. Most people outside The Wealth Center did not believe any man could live up to such high standards and high expectations. They would all be proven wrong!*

Her Lisa would have a Healthy and Wealthy Self-Image, not to mention an Unprecedented, Unheard of, Uncommon, and Unique High Self-Worth and High Self-Identity. And when it was time for her wedding day, she would get married to a <u>Good Man who treated her like the lady, queen, princess, and Phenomenal Woman she was born to celebrate every day of her life.</u> *Self-Respect was everything, and her daughter would be Full of That. Mary and Jason would see to it!!!*

In fact, it started on the first day of The Wealth Training.

Additionally, Mary and Jason had gone out of their way too purchase baby monitors so they could hear their Lisa, no matter which room she, or anyone else was in. If Lisa only knew how much she was loved. Her every motion, sound, and energy would be heard and captured.

Also, Mary and Jason had done lots of research on what to expect during each stage of their daughter's Early Childhood Development, and Mary thought that it would be nice to hang a brightly colored mobile over the crib for Lisa to see, play with, and appreciate. Children are fascinated with colors, and having the mobile in the nursery would help Lisa develop an acute and Advanced Level of Curiosity about the world she lived in. <u>Lisa would always be stimulated by new ideas</u>.

New baby clothes fit for a little Wealthy Princess had been purchased as well. Every woman is a Daughter of the Most High God, and Lisa would not play the part, she would be the part!!! God does not want his girls looking any less. Yes, dressing modestly like the Bible says is important, but Mary and Jason would put their own personal spin and interpretation on the true definition of modesty.

The church world would have you to believe that a female has a Jezebel (whorish) spirit if she wears makeup, jewelry, or nail polish. In a world where women are abused verbally, physically, sexually, and financially, to the point where they feel de-valued as a female and as human beings, they need to know that is okay to be a lady. Unless you would rather for a female to dress like a tomboy so you will not feel sexually threatened by how beautiful she really is.

It is okay, or at least it should be okay, for a female that is single to safely celebrate being a woman without some weak, lustful man or an insecure, envious, and jealous married woman making , mean,shrewd comments or off the wall remarks to deliberately make her feel anything less than a <u>Phenomenal Woman of God</u>!!! It is time for double standards concerning woman anywhere to be totally done away with. Single men are not viewed as a threat. They can put on a suit and tie, and everyone thinks he is Jesus. But, he may have beaten his girlfriend up last night, if he has one. Or he might have two or three on the side, just for sport.

For some reason or another, it is a social taboo for a single female to be single. It is okay to <u>Celebrate your Femininity</u> without being made to feel like you are a disgrace to the human race, simply because you are not married.

Mary and Jason had done a lot of talking about their future since coming to The Wealth Center, and Jason had vowed he would always spend time letting his Lisa know how special she was. He would send her roses, buy her candy, give her cards "just because," for no particular reason, and he would give her money for what she needed and for some of the things she wanted, and speak respectfully to her to send her a message of what it actually means to be treated like a lady. Their daughter would not be raised to take care of a man because he is too lazy or too financially irresponsible to take care of his business at home or abroad.

Jason would cook a special meal for his Lisa, and sit her down to a romantic dinner often, so she would know that these are the kinds of things that a real man does for that special someone in his life. His Lisa would not attract dead-beat men who only use women as a bank or punching bag.

Chapter Twelve

THE PHENOMENAL WOMEN'S CONFERENCE

Mary thought to herself, "Perhaps Jason and I can go to a maternity store tomorrow so I can purchase some new outfits." She phoned down to the lobby for Paul, the chauffeur to set up the trip.

Mary wanted to make certain that she looked good and smelled good throughout her pregnancy. She would Pass This Genetic Gift on to her precious Lisa. Every day of her life, Lisa would <u>Look Good</u> and <u>Smell Good</u>.

Here at The Wealth Center, there would be plenty of cologne for her husband, plenty of perfume for her, and plenty of baby lotion and other good-smelling things that her Lisa would need with each passing year.

Shopping for Maternity clothes was a huge success. Mary found all the perfect outfits and fashion accessories that matched her new inner beauty. Jason was thrilled with all her selections. His wife was "stepping into her own." Being a mother looked good on Mary. Each step she took, and each decision she made was having a Positive Impact upon their bundle of joy.

"Coming to The Wealth Center was the best thing they had ever done. If only the whole world could have such fortune. "But, was that not the very reason they were here?" Jason thought – "to teach the world that no matter what station you are in life that you can get there from here?"

"Speaking of stations," Jason thought, "perhaps it might be appropriate for his beloved wife, Mary, to sponsor a baby shower, so that everyone could lend all their emotional support to her during such a momentous occasion. After all, this was Mary's first pregnancy, and she should be surrounded by her family and friends. He was quite sure Mary would be pleased." He was right, of course!

Mary had gotten so caught up in planning for the baby shower until The Wealth Center staff thought she would over-exert herself. That would not be good for the baby. But, Mary's adrenaline was pumping and she was Deliriously Happy!!! Jason was surprised at what happened next.

"Jason," said Mary, "we have been extremely blessed beyond measure." "Eye hath not seen, nor ear heard, neither have entered into the heart of man the things which God hath prepared for them that love him. But God hath revealed them unto us by His Spirit" (1 Corinthians 2:9-10)…"If there is anything I have learned since being here at The Wealth Center, it is how to <u>think outside the box</u>."

"As you know, it is customary for women to provide baby showers for expectant mothers. Everyone usually shows up and showers the mother with lots of gifts. Jason, why not do something different? We could have a Phenomenal Women's Conference, instead, where we shower Lisa with the gift of knowing what it means to be surrounded by women of Uncommon Virtue, Dignity, and High Self-Worth.

For example, remember when I told you I used to go to the beach in Kennebunkport, Maine, and lose myself in books? I guess you could say, I literally grew up Reading all the Bible stories that highlighted women like Mary, the mother of Jesus, Elizabeth, the mother of John the Baptist, Anna the Prophetess, Esther, Ruth, Naomi, the Virtuous woman in Proverbs 31, Eve, Sarah, just to name a few. I never tired of Reading these stories, and I want to pass this tradition down to Lisa. <u>That will be our Legacy to her.</u> <u>And in turn, she can pass that Legacy on to her own children.</u>"

Jason finally got a chance to get a word in. "That is an excellent idea, Mary! I am grateful for the Wealth Center's life-long training, but someone might think that we are just here for the money, and that all this training is nothing more than just a waste of time. You cannot put a price tag on human worth and virtue.

Go ahead and make all the arrangements. Perhaps you should start planning the guest list and the itinerary for your Phenomenal Women's Conference. In the meantime, I have some plans I need to make as well. Of course, Mary would never know what he had planned for her until the day of the Conference. She would be surprised, and she would never see it coming. This was his opportunity to make good on a promise he had made to his wife. And this surprise would only be the first of many!"

You Are A Phenomenal Woman,

And You Have Been Cordially Invited

To Attend Lisa Lee Chancellor's

Baby Shower (First Phenomenal Women's Conference/Weekend Retreat)

To Be Held At The Wealth Center

From Friday, March 20th - Sunday, March 22nd

Your Carriage (White Stretch Limo) will pick you up on Friday, at 5:00p.m. Sharp!

And Will Transport You Home at 10:00 p.m. on Sunday

Wear Something Comfortable/ No Luggage or Personal Accessories Necessary!

Come And See What Phenomenon Awaits You,

As We Celebrate Our Beloved Daughter!

Please RSVP by Wednesday, March 16th

(708) 888-9999

Mary could not wait until the women received this invitation. They had no idea just how Special this day would be for all of them! Mary knew that all her family and friends would go out of the way to find the Perfect Gift for such a fabulous occasion, but they had no idea what gifts awaited them! Mary was about to take this baby shower/ Phenomenal Women's Conference/weekend retreat to a whole new level. Every woman would leave The Wealth Center feeling like a Queen.

March 21st finally arrived, and Mary Could Not Be Happier!!! As soon as the ladies arrived, they were to be taken to the Registration Area of the Lobby to check in, receive their itineraries, and obtain their room assignments for the duration of their stay. Next, they would all be escorted to The Wealth Center's Convention Center to receive a very hearty welcome by Mary herself.

"Ladies, I bid you a hearty welcome. You cannot imagine how delighted I am to see each one of you. Your presence here means the world to me. Obviously, you read the invitation I sent to you, and you know that it is customary for ladies to get together during bridal showers to shower the mother-to-be with gifts. But as you will soon discover, this is not an ordinary event. This is most definitely not an ordinary baby shower.

I am sure you are pretty tired from the trip, which I hope you enjoyed. But for right now, I am asking each and every one of you to go upstairs and locate your rooms, so that you can get freshened up for dinner. Once you are settled in, several of The Wealth Center staff will take you into another part of the wing where you will find a room full of evening gowns and evening wear and all the accessories you need to "dress for the occasion" for the remainder of your stay. Dinner will be promptly served at 7:30 p.m. At that time, you will have a chance to learn more about the place Jason and I live, and why we all are here at this moment in our lives. God Speed!!!"

One by one, the women excitedly filed out of the room, wondering what this weekend had in store for them. They had Millions of questions, but no one dared speak. Everyone had the feeling that this was more than a fairytale ending. This seemed much too real.

The ladies were chatting with one another loudly as their eyes beheld the Convention Center's surroundings. They all had seen Opulence and Luxury, but not on this scale! They all were very well traveled, yet they had never seen anything this Spectacular! Many speculated on how or why Mary and Jason, of all people, were here. It was common knowledge that Mary and Jason had been anything but Wealthy. Yet, here was Mary hosting her first Women's Conference!

Soft Music had been playing in the background, but everyone became silent when Dr. Lemar Rich took center stage to start the presentation slides. By the time the presentation slides had been presented, there was not a dry eye in the room. They all Understood the Impact the Wealth Center's Training would not only have on Mary, Jason, and Lisa, but the world.

This weekend would be an Unforgettable Phenomenon. And all Mary and Jason's family and friends had been Chosen To Participate in this life-changing moment. As soon as everyone had stepped foot into the limo at 5:00 p.m., their Wealth Training had begun. They would never see life in the same way. As everyone enjoyed the meal, they all were privy to all the pictures that Mary and Jason had taken since moving into The Wealth Center. Those pictures had been captured on the wonderful technology that Mary would never be able to explain in a thousand years.

Tomorrow, during the two hour break immediately following lunch, Mary would give a tour of The Wealth Center to her beloved family and friends. They still had no idea how GIFTED they would be when they left the facility – in more ways than one!

At 7:00 am the next morning, Mary and all the ladies got dressed for breakfast. But each woman had the option of going down into the dining area to partake of a festive feast, or ordering room service. The Wealth Center understood and assumed, not to mention presumed, that on an occasion such as this that it would be appropriate for each guest to pre-order their meals by filling out the menu cards.

During this retreat, every lady, whether taking her breakfast in her room or in the Convention Center area, <u>Would Have The luxury</u> of ordering anything their heart desired – from something as simple as an egg biscuit, fruit and yogurt, or a flat out continental breakfast which consisted of anything on or not on the menu.

Of course, The Wealth Center was not about to tell anyone, especially Mary and Jason, that this method of serving breakfast was merely part of the Wealth Study. If put in a situation where she can have as little or as much food as possible, what would each female select? In some cases, most people might think that it would be appropriate to eat as little as possible. Perhaps others might eat more than usual.

Why did it matter how much anyone ate? The Wealth Center's job is to <u>Promote Wealth On Every Human And Spiritual Plane Possible, and it was important to get that message into the psyche of each participant.</u> On average, it is assumed that one will show politeness during an outing in any place other than home, and only eat the minimal amount of food.

In this case, it is the Wealth Center's point of view that a person who eats less than more, for whatever reason, has a poverty thinking spirit (a spirit where there is not enough to go around). Here at The Wealth Center, and in God's Universe, <u>there is more than enough to go around</u>. That is the message that everyone at The Wealth Center was trying to endorse. No one should have to wrestle with the fear of "running out!" Such fear in the long run will only lead to lack and limitation.

Breakfast had been served, and everyone was in a hurry for the Phenomenal Women's Conference to begin. Each woman had awakened to exquisite toiletries, delicate accessories, top notch makeup kits, creams, lotions, perfumes exported directly from Paris, pantyhose, shoes, and everything they needed to prepare for their busy, but Phenomenal and Productive day. All each woman had to do this morning was tell her personal assistant which designer gown or dress she wanted to wear.

It could have been said that dressing formally each day during this Conference was ridiculous. But, this was not a casual event, and no one wanted to come to Lisa's First Phenomenal Women's Conference adorned in anything less than astoundingly Wealthy. Lisa had not yet been born, but she was aware of her mother's surroundings at all times. This Special Moment was being captured on video, and someday when

Lisa was old enough, she would be shown these pictures of how everyone was dressed.

Here, at The Wealth Center, Lisa would be anything but casual. She was <u>Destined For Greatness</u>, and she would always dress like she was the Daughter of the Most High God, Jehovah. <u>God is the center of everyone's Wealth, and Lisa would be the part.</u>

"Who can find a virtuous woman? For her price is far above rubies. The heart of her husband doth safely trust in her, so that he shall have no need of spoil. She will do him good and not evil all the days of her life. She seeketh wool, and flax,and worketh willingly with her hands. She is like the merchants' ships; she bringeth her food from afar. She riseth also while it is yet night, and giveth meat to her household, and a portion to her maidens. She considereth a field and and buyeth it: With the fruit of her hands she planteth a vineyard. She girdeth her loins with strength, and strengtheneth her arms. She perceiveth that her merchandise is good: her candle goeth out not by night. She layeth her hands to the spindle, and her hands hold the distaff. She stretcheth out her hand to the poor; yea, she reacheth forth her hands to the needy. She is not afraid of the snow for her household: for all her household are clothed with scarlet. She maketh maketh herself coverings of tapestry; her clothing is silk and purple. Her husband is known in the gates, when he sitteth among the elders of the land. She maketh fine linen, and selleth it; and delivereth girdles unto the merchant. Strength and honour are her clothing; and she shall rejoice in time to come. She openeth her mouth with wisdom; and in her tongue is the law of kindness. She looketh well to the ways of her household, and eateth not the bread of idleness. Her children arise up, and call her blessed; her husband also, and he praiseth her. Many daughters have done virtuously, but thou excellest them all. Favor is deceitful, and beauty is vain: but a woman that feareth the Lord, she shall be praised. Give her of the fruit of her hands; and let her own works praise her in the gates" (Proverbs 31:10-31).

Everyone cried as Jasmine, Mary's sister, completed the Scripture Reading. She read it with so much emotion and depth. Mary and Jason knew their Lisa was allowing these words to Saturate her Mind, Body, Soul and Spirit. Lisa was surrounded by virtuous woman who had passed on that Seed of Virtue to her.

Next, Mary's cousin, Samantha, stepped up into the pulpit to recite this Scripture, "A good name is rather to be chosen than great riches" (Proverbs 22:1). Mary was beside herself at this point, and was obviously very emotional. She and her beloved husband, Jason, had not taken their daughter's name lightly. That is why they spent over three hours selecting the Perfect Name for their daughter. Her Name had to reflect God's Character and Nature, first and foremost. Secondly, it had to reflect their journey before and after The Wealth Center. And lastly, it had to reflect the Jewel their daughter would become. God loves His girls and he wants every girl to feel as <u>Unique</u> as her Name. Their Lisa would teach seceding girls how Special they were!

Meanwhile, Jason had his own personal agenda. He would surprise his wife with a surprise fashion show. As an artist, he had a few contacts that would be more than happy to make this Phenomenal Women's Conference the Greatest Meeting anyone had ever sponsored. Jason was not showing off by such a gesture. He wanted to help his wife, his "help meet," (Genesis 2:18) put the "Phenomenon into "Phenomenal." He felt it was his duty as a man to demonstrate to both men and women how that Phenomenon could actually lead to <u>Healthier Relationships between husbands and wives</u>.

Jason had invited a large number of celebrity models to come to The Wealth Center to model top of the line gowns, formal wear, bridal gowns, and attire that would put the Richest Princess and Queen to shame. Jason had been taken captive by his wife's beauty, and he was absolutely fascinated with the Scripture found in Isaiah 61:3: "The garment of praise for the spirit of heaviness…" If praise was a measure of one's beauty or Wealth, his "girls" would wear that particular garment exceptionally well.

He would deliberately throw this kind of garment into the picture, so to speak, to promote the idea that "<u>Great is the Lord and Greatly to be Praised; and His Greatness is Unsearchable</u>" (Psalm 145:3)!!! He had also come to believe, since being at The Wealth Center, that every female should enhance and accentuate her positives. A woman should go out of her way to feel feminine and pretty!

He believed that each woman, like Queen Esther – his wife's favorite role model - should dress so well she keeps her husband's undivided attention. Most men are known for wanting their leading lady to <u>look stunning</u>!!! Jason was in that category. His wife would never look like a slouch. The same went for his Lisa!

By the time this Elegant, Luxurious, Phenomenal Women's Conference was over, every lady in attendance would know his preference for this Phenomenon as well, which he deemed nothing short of artistic.

This Conference was Jason's way of combining his love for art with the science of making every woman feel beautiful from the inside out. Every lady, courtesy of Jason Jewel Chancellor, would be leaving The Wealth Center with an Inestimable array of gowns and dresses that were specifically designed to bring out her natural and Supernatural essence. Every woman would leave his castle Feeling like a Princess! That would be his Trademark and Legacy that he would want to share with every man in the world. Everyone would think he was a Jewel!!!

After a fabulous power luncheon, Mary escorted the women on a tour of the Campus. All her friends knew that she and Jason had moved into The Wealth Center, but up to this point, no one had actually been there to visit.

Mary's family was exceptionally busy taking care of their husbands and children, and pursuing their own areas of interest, and Mary and Jason had been heavily engaged with the Wealth Programming and the excitement of having their first child. No one had time to visit anyone.

That was why this time was Special to Mary. She was surrounded by her family, and this was her first time to make a good impression. She had arrived! She was Feeling Successful, unlike other times in her life when everyone wondered why she could not seem to "get it together," especially after living in such a Rich Environment.

Mary was very proud to share this moment and her new home with her family. Family was everything!!! That was the True Meaning Of Wealth!!! One could have all the Money in the world, but if they had no real friends or family to share in that Success, life would be totally meaningless. This tour meant everything to Mary!!! She could show off what she had learned as a result of being here at The Wealth Center.

Mary was proud of her newly developed and newly founded interior decorating skills and she could not wait to show off the Elegance, Beauty and Splendor of her surroundings to all the ladies. She was especially proud of "The Gold Room."

She spent a lot of time finding the perfect gold drapes, the perfect white carpeting, the perfectly golden antique furniture, and the perfect accessories that would highlight how she and her family had <u>Struck Gold</u>. Her most prized possession was the <u>knight in shining armor</u>, which highlighted the Ephesians 6 (Putting On The Whole Armor Of God Scripture). It had been replicated in solid gold to remind her "to stand against the wiles of the devil (Ephesians 6:10), meaning to protect herself from any evil force that would make her feel unworthy of all the Wealth God had given her. Anyone who stepped into this room got the Feeling they were walking down the Streets of Gold in Heaven as mentioned in Revelation 21.

Next, Mary chose to go into The Meditation Room that she had set apart as her Peaceful Sanctuary which she had personally and deliberately decorated alone. She had been a bundle of nerves before she came here to The Wealth Center, and she had Created a haven that would make her Feel Out Of This World!!! Perhaps this was a direct reflection of all the time she spent alone in Maine – just soaking in the atmosphere.

As soon as you stepped into this room, the first thing you could hear was the sounds of a waterfall. If you looked up into the high, skyline of a glass ceiling, you could feel the warmth of the sun's rays. No matter where you were in this room, the sun could be felt from head to toe.

Mary's family Bible that she had often taken with her to the beach in Maine rested on a gold table that was so transparent, you could see yourself in all that gold. This room was so treasured by Mary that everyone in The Wealth Center knew to leave her alone with her thoughts, no matter how long she was in there. Someone on the staff always found the time to put up a "Please do not disturb sign" if Mary forgot to do so. Everyone respected Mary's boundaries, including Jason.

Next, Mary took the ladies out through the gardens, past the gazebo, to show them the Unprecedented and Unparalleled Library. The room itself was almost bigger than the Library of Congress. The women had time to browse through some of the books that were housed in these quarters.

Mary trusted everyone who decided to check out some of the books to bring them back in the same condition they were in before they left the premises. She knew the Principles contained within the books would serve them all well in the future. Pretty soon, the Early Childhood Education world, those who worked in Prenatal Care, and those who worked in any capacity with children of any age, or any human and social service agency dedicated to Family Services would be bombarded with these books in the effort to replicate and duplicate their teachings.

Mary felt like these books and Wealth Tapes were taking her back into her Mother's Womb (John 3:4) all over again so she could re-capture what she thought she had lost. This Wealth Study would give many children a second head start and give others their first chance to get it right the first time around (Programming Loved Ones For Wealth). Perhaps this Study's Principles were so Universal in nature, other non-Wealth topics of interest could be substituted. Who knows what kind of impact this Wealth Study would have on society and the whole world as a whole. Mary felt like a pioneer. Perhaps she and Jason were setting a new trend in thought.

After the tour, everyone took advantage of the two-hour break. For those who wanted a more advanced tour, one of the staff members were on hand to provide that Luxury. They did not want to tire Mary out. She needed her rest. After all, the campus was much too big for Mary to try to give the complete tour herself.

On Sunday, the final day of these festivities, Jason had one more Pleasant Surprise to spring on Mary and her guests. Remember the fashion show with the bridal gowns? In this respect, Jason had pulled a fast one on all the women including Mary. No one figured out that Jason was presenting a hint as to his Future Intentions to Make Good on the Promise he made to himself.

While Mary had been busy planning the Conference, Jason and his buddies had been planning a Formal Proposal. He would get down on his knee, right in front of Mary and all the ladies and ask her to marry him all over again. This time around, he would give Mary the wedding she wanted and deserved!!!

Jason had spent weeks looking at the Perfect Wedding Ring for this momentous occasion. Mary was none the wiser that some of the women who were coming to The Wealth Center were not all celebrity models. Many of them were women coming and going with Mary's choice ring – a ring that was to meet the approval of Jason's Exquisite Eye for detail, and flair for brilliantly sophisticated lines.

Of course, Mary had no idea that Jason had never left campus during the Conference. He had been in his Phenomenal Man's Conference, sharing with his friends, family, and business associates many of the Techniques that he had learned since being at The Wealth Center. Jason would share that information with Mary on a later day. But today was a different story!!! Jason had a PROPOSAL to make and he would not keep his wife waiting!!!

Mary was enjoying the festivities when Daphne walked ever so gently into the room to alert Mary to a couple of details that had to be taken care of immediately. Mary was told to come down to The Wealth Center Lobby to attend to an urgent matter that only she could handle.

As Mary was standing in the lobby trying to track down what was so urgent that only she could take care of it, Jason had entered into the Conference Room and let everyone in on his secret. He had asked one of the Wealth Center staff members to bring in a large Christmas tree to be placed in the corner of the Conference Room.

The guests were asked to put any baby shower gifts underneath the tree.

This Christmas tree was significant. Jason had Proposed to Mary on Christmas Day, and he would Propose to her again, giving Mary the illusion that this Phenomenal Women's Conference was actually Christmas Day. Since being here at The Wealth Center, both Mary and Jason had learned how to <u>Think Outside The Box</u>, alleviating many of the traditions they were accustomed to. They had learned to Celebrate any moment of any day at the drop of a hat.

At The Wealth Center, Lisa would learn, if she had not gotten the message inside her Mother's Womb already, that it is possible to Celebrate major holidays during any day of the week. Normal people celebrate Christmas on December 25th, but Lisa might decide to celebrate Christmas in June or July.

If Lisa wanted to adopt the theme: "365 days of Christmas," where she left up a Christmas tree in her house for one whole year, opening gifts during each of those days, no one would stop her. On the same token, if Lisa Felt Led To Celebrate Thanksgiving three times a year, she would be free to do so. At The Wealth Center, there would always be something to Celebrate!

Mary hurriedly entered the Conference Room, intent on catching up on what information she missed while down in the lobby. She could never figure out why she was not needed downstairs in the foyer. When she got down to the lobby, no one was there. Mary thought that odd!!!

Mary was in such a rush to get back into Conference Mode, she never saw the Christmas tree. In fact, she never saw Jason!!! One minute, she was listening to one of the speakers discussing one of the Phenomenal Women of the Bible, and the next minute, Jason was walking up to her smiling from ear to ear.

"Mary, I know you are probably wondering why I am here at this exact moment, but actually I have been here at The Wealth Center the whole time this Conference was in session, conducting my own session with all the Phenomenal Men that are in this room right now." Mary never saw any men in the room, but as she looked around, she saw all of them sitting contently in the back of the conference room.

"Mary," Jason continued, "There is a reason I am here. I love you so very much. You are the Love Of My Life and I will love you forever. But, I was not financially capable of giving you the wedding day that you deserved, yet you married me anyway." "Today," said Jason, as he got down on one knee, "I want to change all that. I want to give you the wedding ceremony you always wanted. Mary, will you marry me all over again. I promise this time, we will get it right!"

Mary tried to fight back the tears welling up in her eyes, but she let them flow instead. Jason was Proposing to her in front of all these people.

She looked at the new engagement ring Jason had slipped on her finger just now. It was the ring she had always wanted – a large, shiny, yellow gold band with a spectacularly large diamond. It looked good on her finger. Mary tried not to faint as she said, "Yes, I will marry you, Jason Jewel Chancellor."

Everyone in the room was standing up on their feet, applauding loudly. Many of the women were crying. The men were patting each other on the back. It had taken a journey for Mary and Jason to get to this place! Without thinking, Mary hugged Jason with all her strength. He held her back with the same vigor and passion. They could not let each other go!!! <u>For them, Time Had Stood Still</u>. This moment would be forever embedded upon their memories – and Lisa's. <u>One day, Lisa would know this kind of endless bliss!</u>

After this Special Moment, almost as if they knew, everyone sat down and remained absolutely still and silent. They wanted to allow this Special Moment to take full effect. If there was ever a time to move with "The Spirit," it was now! No one wanted to move. And no one did move, for about thirty minutes.

Jason broke the silence by walking to the front of the Conference Room. This was the perfect moment to read excerpts from Lisa Lee Hairston's Lady's Devotional: *You Are A Jewel.*

Jason said, "Ladies, I think it befitting that I take this time to read you a few excerpts from the book, *You Are A Jewel!* I think it best sums up this Phenomenal Women's Conference. It was written by Lisa Lee Hairston. I dedicate these words to my lovely wife, my Mary, and to all of you. You are absolutely remarkable!!!"

You Are Adorable!

God absolutely and unequivocally adores you, and he finds you irresistibly adorable. He worships the ground you walk on!

You Are Alive!

You were not born by accident. You were planned by God, and conceived in His mind before He planted you in your mother's womb. You are Heaven's destiny and earth's finest treasure. He "breathed His life into your nostrils and you became a living soul – his soul (Genesis). And you bring life to God's world. You are alive and well!

You Are Awesome!

Believe me when I tell you that you have it going on! And God is undoubtedly in awe of you. God is awestruck. I just thought you should know. God wants you to be His First Lady, His Queen, and the Love of his Life! He wants to make you His!

You Are Beautiful!

In case someone has never told you this, you blow God's mind! Your stunningly, exquisite beauty takes Jehovah God's breath away. You are exquisitely beautiful from the inside out. God will never exploit that beauty. After all, He created it. You are beautiful!

You Are Bright!

The Universe is your playground. You are brighter than the sun, brighter than the moon, and brighter than the stars. Your brightness is a beacon to those who have yet to come to the Light. You are the brightness of God's Glory!

You Are Brilliant!

Jehovah God is infatuated with your brilliance. God respects your mind. He loves the way you think. Amazingly, God "gets you, even if others do not. You are God's soul mate. How does it feel to be gotten by God?

You Are Creative!

You were created for such a time as this, to allow the Goddess in you to come forth for others to behold the image of God in you. Let it be said of you, "She is the spitting image of Jehovah God. When I got her, I got the best! You have God's creative power in you, and you have the power to create and re-create (recreation) a perfect world in your world, which is tied up, wrapped up, and tangled up in Jehovah God. You are absolutely creative!

You Are Dazzling!

When Moses came down off Mount Sinai after God had given him the Ten Commandments, his face was shining so brightly, he had no choice but to wear a veil when he spoke to God's people face to face. Consequently, you are so dazzling to Jehovah God that He wants to remove your wedding veil so that others can see just how dazzling you are to Him. Who knew you were that dazzling?

You Are Deep!

You belong to Jehovah God, as His choice bride, therefore, there is nothing shallow about you! There is nothing superficial about you. You are not as transparent or as predictable as everyone thought. There is more to you than meets the eye. There is that part of you, which is beneath the surface that is reserved only for Jehovah God - for His eyes only – for his ears only – for his touch only.

You Are Divine!

God is not a man that he should lie, therefore, he will never hurt you, leave you, let you down, or break your heart. That is what separates man's humanity from Christ's Divinity. When it comes to giving you "good love," the "real deal," and the "real thing" God puts the Doctor in Divinity (D.Div). "In God's Divinity, you can trust." You are absolutely Divine!

You Are Fair!

Jesus is the "fairest of ten thousand" and so are you. No one knew that you were that fair! Your fairness is beyond everyone's imagination or human intellect. When anyone encounters you in any capacity, you leave them with the sense that they have been in the Presence of Almighty God who will treat them more fairly than they expected. What a powerful testimony!

You Are Fantastic!

God is your number one fan and that is why he puts the "Fan" in your fantastic!!! You are his "biggest hit!" God has made you His shining star. You are on his number one list. Even at this moment, God is giving you "Rave Reviews!!!"

"At this time, I would like to present The Wealth Center's Wealth Center staff who are more than happy to present you with a free, complimentary copy of the book I just read from. Hopefully, you will leave The Wealth Center Feeling Like A Jewel. <u>You are priceless.</u>"

After Jason's Reading, it was time for the unwrapping of the gifts. For the first time, Mary saw the Christmas tree, with all the beautiful lights. The Christmas tree was no match for her eyes lighting up. Mary was overcome with joy!!!

One by one, the women presented their gifts to Mary as she sat in front of the room. Of course, every woman in the room had wondered what gifts to buy for Mary and the baby since Mary and Jason were now a part of The Wealth Center. They appeared to have it all. But it was the thought that counts, and everyone conducted themselves as if it were a normal baby shower by buying items that any mother and child might want and need.

For Mary, this presentation of gifts was more than a baby shower moment. She felt as though it was Christmas and that she was opening up all the gifts under the tree for the first time. She was as delighted as a child to open each wrapped gift.

There were state-of-the-art cooking utensils, pots and pans, deep fryers, crock pots, pasta makers, microwaves, woks, as well as perfumes, lotions, jewelry, and other items that Mary would like. For Lisa, there were lots of booties, dresses, pampers, hair bows, hair accessories, etcetera. During this moment, the presentation of the baby shower gifts was caught on tape. This event was just another reminder to Lisa (yet to be born) that real Wealth is Infinite. If one would Dare To Believe, Wealth is one commodity that will never run out. <u>There is Plenty of Infinite Wealth To Go Around For Everyone,</u> which is what every woman attending this Phenomenal Women's Conference discovered.

By Sunday, all of the women had come to believe that fairytales can and will come true. During the last day of the Conference, (March 22), the women met one last time in the Convention Center for one final breakfast together. Mary and Jason would spend the remainder of the day ensuring that each woman had been graced with the assortment of gowns, formal evening wear, and accessories they were to be GIFTED with before they were to leave The Phenomenal Women's Conference – gifts that would put Queen Sheba or any other Queen to shame. Every woman would leave the facilities knowing that anything was possible. After all, it was Mary and Jason's aim to Promote the Wealth they had come into unexpectedly as a result of being Chosen to Participate In The Wealth Study.

Final goodbyes were spoken before each woman got into her particular limo on Sunday night at 10:00 p.m. to travel back to her respective home, but not before everyone had agreed that they would all come together in Perfect Unity later to Celebrate the Thanksgiving holidays. Everyone was already looking forward to what was just around the corner. Somehow they knew that "God was saving the best for last!!!"

Chapter Thirteen

THE ROMANTIC PICNIC FOR TWO

Day after day, Mary, Jason, and the entire Wealth Center staff went out of their way to maintain a Healthy and Wealthy Atmosphere for Lisa. They continued Reading to Lisa and playing all the tapes. It would not be long before their Lisa would arrive.

Jason wanted to spend as much time alone with Mary before Lisa was born. He arranged a picnic away from The Wealth Center. He and the chef, Jeffrey, planned the perfect menu for he and Mary to enjoy during their "alone time." They would feast and dine on potato salad, baked beans, croissants, a salad tossed with fresh spinach and arugula, tomatoes with oil and vinegar, baked chicken, chocolate raspberry cheesecake, and freshly squeezed lemonade.

Mary and Jason talked for hours after a pleasant meal. They had never had so much fun! Jason could not remember when he and Mary had had this much enjoyment. He loved to make Mary laugh, and laugh she did. They just lost themselves in the moment as they released every inhibition, especially Mary. With respect to her personality, Mary was the more reserved of the two, but not today!

One would think that Mary was a child again, taking advantage of every single adventure. One would have also thought that Mary was acting out of character. He, of all people, knew his wife better than anyone, and he had never seen Mary this Happy!!! But perhaps it was the confession that she had made to him during today's rendez-vous that had triggered such a pleasant reaction in her. Mary had worked up the nerve to tell him that she could never love any other man the way she loved him. Up to this point, Jason had never known that Mary's intention was to spend the rest of her life showing him how much she loved him, starting today. Mary had been too shy to say anything about her feelings for him before. She loved him beyond words, but she never said the actual words, "I love you," out loud. That was about to change!!!

Perhaps it was the Wealthy Atmosphere at The Wealth Center that brought out the best in Mary – or perhaps it was the fact that Mary was about to be a new mother – that sparked in her the deep, intimate need to reach out to her husband to give him Zillions of hugs and kisses every day!!! After all, they were husband and wife, and Mary just thought that before and after Lisa's Birth, she and Jason should never lose sight of their love for one another. Yes, having a baby does change things, but that should never get in the way of a husband and wife "making time" for one another. Mary believed that if she spent <u>Quality Time</u> alone with Jason every day, there would be more love to share with their daughter. Lisa was after all their Love Child that was Conceived in Love!!!

Jason vowed at the moment of Mary's confession to spend more "alone time" with her before and after Lisa was born. Now was the Perfect Time for him and Mary to begin the new tradition of what they called, "Date Night!!!" Every Monday, for the rest of their lives, Mary and Jason would spend the whole day and night together alone, regardless of what their schedules merited. Everyone would know how much Jason loved his wife. Mary was his top priority!

Mary and Jason took a lot of pictures, as had been the custom since moving into The Wealth Center. Thankfully, someone from The Wealth Center had packed both their photo albums and wedding albums into some tote bag when items for the picnic were being placed in the trunk of the limo earlier this morning. Someone had put Jason's art supplies into the trunk as well, just in case he was inspired to paint, which he was.

There was one painting in Jason's mind that he had on the back burner. As he began to paint Mary on the canvas, he added one special touch

– her wedding gown – the one she wanted but could not afford. <u>He was as deeply in love with his wife today as he was on the day he married her,</u> and he captured the beauty of her wedding day as he remembered her on his beloved canvas. And he would hang his wife's Portrait that he painted today at the entrance of their living room at The Wealth Center for their Lisa to see. <u>He was the Wealthiest man alive in more ways than one. He would cherish this moment forever</u>!!!

Chapter Fourteen

THE THANKSGIVING DINNER

Jason loved his wife, Mary, beyond words, yet he knew Mary would insist on cooking the entire Thanksgiving meal herself, being that Thanksgiving Day was undoubtedly her favorite holiday, hands down! Therefore his wife would try to oversee the whole meal and take care of the baby if they chose to celebrate the happy festivities on the traditional Thanksgiving Day. By that time in November, their baby would only be a little more than a month old.

Jason thought it would be best if the family got together to Celebrate the holiday on the third Thursday in July, before the baby was born. At least on that day, they could all just focus on Pampering Mary and enjoy looking forward to Lisa's Birth – which was the family's primary reason for surrounding Mary with <u>so much love</u>

and positive energy. They all wanted to ensure that Mary had a Healthy Delivery. They did not want her to over exert herself in any way.

This was Mary and Jason's first Thanksgiving living at The Wealth Center, however, they chose to celebrate the holidays with family and friends at their previous home, which was two hours away. Jason had left strict instructions with the Wellington's as to his expectations for the day. Under no circumstances was Mary to try to cook the whole Thanksgiving dinner herself. Jason would insist that Mary kick her feet up and Relax as much as possible throughout the whole day.

Mary had set her heart on cooking the 21-pound turkey by herself, but when Jason phoned Mrs. Wellington, he asked her to have the turkey fully defrosted before their arrival. That way, all Mary had to do was baste the turkey with her warm, melted garlic butter sauce, and put it into the oven to roast for a few hours.

At first, Mary had felt put out about Jason's decision for her to rest. She fought against Jason's idea of taking it easy, but he was her husband, and she desperately wanted to please him like the Bible said, especially on such a glorious day, but she concluded that if she conceded in this matter, everyone would benefit from a Win-Win situation. After all, she would still be in charge of cooking the turkey, the macaroni and cheese, and gravy. Jason would feel like he had saved the day. And all their guests could enjoy one another's company, Great Conversation, and the bundle of joy that was about to make her grand entrance into the family and into God's lovely world on Friday, October 13th.

On the morning of the Thanksgiving Dinner, Jason, who had always been an early riser, had gotten up at 5:00 a.m. to bring Mary breakfast in bed. They were to be leaving The Wealth Center at 10:30 a.m., and Jason wanted to make his wife as comfortable as possible before taking on the two-hour drive. He would see to it that she would eat all her "breakfast favorites."

Jason would make Mary fresh chicken salad on a bed of romaine lettuce, and fresh roasted tomatoes with extra virgin olive oil and a pinch of garlic salt. He splashed a generous amount of fresh lemon juice on the chicken salad itself for an extra burst of flavor. Nothing was too good for his Mary! He would also make Mary a small seared tuna steak, drizzled with a twist of fresh lime juice and lime zest. He would finish it off with an exotic fruit salad (fresh pineapple, mandarin oranges, coconut, marshmallows, cream cheese, sour cream, walnuts, and pecans. He also would serve Mary a large glass of freshly squeezed orange juice and a dozen red roses. Mary cried. Jason was <u>the most romantic husband in the world</u>!!! Perhaps he had missed his calling. Maybe he should have been a Relationship Specialist or Marriage Counselor.

Jason had been right. Mary did need to rest after the two-hour drive. She retired to her old room to take a nap, but not before washing and basting the turkey. She stuffed it with her famous stuffing before placing it into the pre-heated oven. For her, making the macaroni and cheese and gravy could easily be made just minutes before the meal was served.

All the family members arrived, slowly but surely, and it was obvious that everyone was excited about Lisa's Birth, especially the children. Lisa appeared to be the main attraction and the center of attention! There were a couple of children who were just learning how to Read, and they each took turns Reading to the unborn baby some of the books their mothers had checked out during the Phenomenal Women's Conference four months ago. When Lisa kicked out of sheer joy and pleasure, the children were delighted! <u>They were learning at a very early age the importance of Reading the Right Books, Saying the Right Words, and Playing the Right Kind Of Tapes To Obtain the Right Educational Results.</u>

Would this same technique work for adults of any age, and would it be as effective? Mary longed to find out. They all were on the cutting age of <u>new discoveries</u> in the educational (academic), psychological, and Prenatal world. If this Phenomenon caught on, anyone of any age, even before birth, would have the capability of tapping into 100% of their brain power after learning the Power of Biblical Wealth Programming.

Just as a woman wanting to become pregnant by artificial insemination could control which man's sperm she might select for such a procedure (Mary herself would not consider this option; she had only read stories about it), parents could sit down and plan the characteristics they would like to Impart to their child(ren). Mary had also Read of how women in such a position had deliberately chosen to be inseminated with the sperm of a man with a High IQ. Others had chosen sperm that represented a man's good looks and social qualities. In such a case, Mary did not believe in such Genetic Implanting as she called it.

Mary had been at The Wealth Center too long and Participated In The Wealth Study too long to believe that anything other than what God originally designed was appropriate. After all, everyone had been Created in the Image of God, therefore why mess with Perfection. Utilizing the Right Programming Methods would guarantee the same results if they were applied. But what if there were connections between Biblical Programming and Genetics that no one had yet thought of? If there were connections, how would she find out? And from whom? Presently, she did not know anyone who was a Genetic Specialist or Genetic Engineer, as she called it.

But in any case, perhaps this Wealth Study would inspire the concept that a parent who wanted a Healthy child would chose to daily infuse their unborn child with Subliminal Tapes and Books pertaining to Perfect Health. Perhaps another parent with a love for foreign languages would deliberately play foreign language tapes to their unborn child to evaluate the effectiveness of

*that kind of programming once their child could
speak.*

*No one would know for sure if such
Programming Techniques at the Wealth would
work until the results of its findings were released
to the public. Her Lisa's birth would play a major
role in the release of those findings. She was sure
of that! Mary was honored to be Chosen to be
selected for this history-changing moment.*

The dinner went off without a glitch. Mary's
turkey was perfect. She was fully rested!!! Jason
had been the <u>doting, devoted husband and future
father</u>. The children felt like the Perfect Role
Model for the baby. The family was <u>thrilled</u> to be
part of such a Great Legacy. And The Wealth
Center staff was Happy that their Wealth Study
was going better than they previously expected,
and they had gone into such a venture with high
expectations from the very start!

All the other previous families had brought
something unique to The Study with respect
to their <u>Willingness to take the Programming
seriously</u>, but only Mary and Jason would be
considered The Wealth Center's "Poster Family."
*In other words, they would stand out from the rest
of the participants forever. Why? Mary and Jason
were "not in it" just for the money, the fame, or
the glory. Mary and Jason sincerely wanted every
family in the world to feel the impact of what true
wealth actually is. They wanted everyone to know
that every person in the world has the power to
Deliberately Impart any message at any time into*

anyone's heart and Spirit before and after birth, in its Highest Form.

Most people would probably view Mary and Jason's stringent, on-going programming as unnatural, unbiblical, and in poor taste because of the Spiritual Laws that were taught in the process, but one's opinion and debates on why these Principles work or do not work will never prevent those Principles from working if diligently and correctly applied.

"Man has gone to the moon, but not one single astronaut could actually move the moon out of its natural position. "If they could they would," Mary thought. So it is with the Wealth Study they were rigorously subjected to on a daily basis. *The sacrifice was worth its weight in gold. Mary and Jason ended up with more than Physical Money and Financial Wealth. They ended up with emotional, mental, social, and academic Wealth they did not previously possess prior to The Wealth Center's Intensive Training.*

This Wealth Training would bring their families and all families everywhere together to <u>Create Greater Wealth for future generations</u>. *And if each generation was as fortunate as Mary and Jason, each of those generations would take that Great Wealth to a Level Unheard Of By Its Predecessors. That was why this Thanksgiving dinner was unlike any other. This Thanksgiving would go International, with Godspeed, in more ways than one!*

Chapter Fifteen

THE BIRTHING ROOM

The day finally came for Lisa's arrival!!! After Mary's water broke, she and Jason were rushed to the West Wing of the Wealth Center to prepare for Lisa's entry into the earth realm. Mary was in labor, therefore, she and her husband were taken into the Birthing Room immediately.

Jason suited up in his hospital gear, as he called it, and got into position to help Mary stay calm, relaxed, and focused. He would not have to do too much along those lines because everything seemed to be in place exactly as it had been rehearsed in Lamaze Class.

Additionally, Mary and Jason had decided from the start to have this Special Delivery videotaped, and caught on camera so Lisa could see it when she got older. This was "the big day," and everyone wanted Lisa to view the video in its entirety to see all the love that went into such a

Great Delivery. Lisa was after all, their Love Child. She was Conceived In Love and she would be Delivered and Birthed In Love.

During one of the former sessions with Dr. Lee, Mary and Jason had discussed the possibility of having a Natural Childbirth in a Natural, Relaxing Setting and Environment. No one wanted to dampen this moment by Delivering Lisa in any other way. Mary wanted to be free of any medications when Lisa was being Delivered, and she did not want to be heavily sedated or asleep during this Natural Process. Mary wanted to remember every single detail of every second.

True to his word, Dr. Lee did allow Classical Music and Wealth Tapes to be played over the intercom so everyone in the Birthing Room could listen to them. Much to everyone's surprise, the Labor Of Love was not long or difficult, and Lisa came into the world via a very easy Delivery and Painless Childbirth.

The Wealth Center staff wondered if such a Delivery was a direct result of the Wealth Programming that Mary, Jason, and Lisa had been subjected to for the past nine months. The staff made a note of this observation for further study. Lisa weighed in at seven pound and seven ounces during Birth, and everyone was ecstatic.

Mother and daughter were doing so well, in fact, until they were released from The Wealth Center's on-campus hospital facility earlier than expected. Again, everyone wondered if this Phenomenon was due to the Wealth Programming.

But, immediately after birth, everyone took into consideration that this was Mary's first time out being a mother, and Dr. Lee suggested that she and Jason remain in the Birthing Room for a few extra days just so they could bond with their little one. Of course the Birthing Room in itself would expedite the bonding.

Mary had remained calm throughout her Delivery, knowing that Jason was there for her. But perhaps the Serenity of the Birthing Room had its impact as well. There was something Soothing about this Room that amazed Mary. Samuel had been effective in helping Mary overcome her fear of the Delivery Process.

She had taken to heart everything he had told her and shown her about this Room – the ocean blue Feel of the Room, a bed that was just as comfortable as the one she and Jason slept on each night in The Wealth Center, the sound of the waterfall in the background, the laptop computer, (which would come in handy later), a few of Jason's art canvasses and supplies, a mini refrigerator supplied with Healthy Snacks, a large screen television, pictures of the ocean, a large photo album with the first few snapshots of Lisa just after birth, and a journal for Mary to write down her thoughts.

Of course, The Wealth Center never attempted to interfere with the bonding process, but, they had their ways of getting close without being seen or without being in the way. They wanted to ensure that they captured everything they needed to guarantee Right Results of their Wealth Study! The world was waiting!!!

Mary was not as Spiritual as Jason, although she had gone to church regularly since her childhood, but since Lisa's birth, Mary began to think quite a bit about the similarities between her Giving Birth to Lisa and Mary Giving Birth to Jesus, the Son of the Most High God. Mary wondered what Mary was filling when she Gave Birth to Jesus in the inn. She wondered what Mary thought about actually Giving Birth to the Messiah. Did angels watch over Jesus during the night? What was it like for Mary, a Virgin, to Enter Into Motherhood at such a young age? Did Mary fuss over the baby Jesus?

During the last few days, Mary was feeling overly protective of Lisa. She was glad that she, Jason, and Lisa had their privacy here in the Birthing Room. She had heard stories of how some babies had literally been taken out of the hospital by individuals that were not parents. Mary felt safe here!!! Her baby was in capable hands.

She had prepared herself for motherhood by Reading as much as she could about Parenting. She had consulted with multiple Parent Resource Centers, but nothing could prepare her for this actual moment. Mary was now a mother, and she would need a lot of help to bring up Lisa in the Right Environment – an Environment which had nothing and everything to do with The Wealth Center. True enough, there were plenty of Wealth Center staff members who would be more than willing to help her with the baby, but they had a job to do.

They would be concerned about everything relating to Parenting being as Humanly Natural as possible, without compromising the End Results of the Wealth Study. The Wealth Center would not want to contaminate this Process or bias the Results in any way. Mary and Jason would have to step up to the plate and conduct business as if there were not a Study when it came to their Lisa. They would rely on their maternal and paternal instincts, as well as the help of their family members, who happened to be present on campus when Lisa was born. The family was obviously ecstatic about these recent events!

Chapter Sixteen

Lisa's Individualized Education Plan (I.E.P.)

Meanwhile, at The Wealth Center, a Deliberate, Planned, and Calculated Change was made to the Wealth Programming Procedures and Methodologies. All the Tapes and books that had been previously used for nine months were replaced with new ones. Tapes other than the Health and Wealth were being substituted.

Lisa became agitated when she heard the new tapes that had nothing to do with the Healthy and Wealthy ones she had listened to for nine months in her Mother's Womb! When the old tapes were brought back out so Lisa could hear them, she was overjoyed. Lisa did the same things with the stories. If someone snuck in a story that had not been Read to Lisa, she would not stop crying until someone Read one of the familiar stories.

Additionally, if a new story was Read to Lisa that included Stories of Wealth, she would remain in a great mood. Lisa would only cry if what she heard <u>was not conducive to the Wealthy Atmosphere Created for her from her Mother's Womb.</u>

Of course, The Wealth Center made note of these findings, which led to some New Developments in the Wealth Study. The Wealth Center called in a leading psychologist, Dr. Michael Wells, to help them <u>develop a More Advanced Course Of Audiovisual Tapes.</u>

They came up with More Advanced Stories concerning Wealth, upgrading the reading comprehension, mathematical and vocabulary/ language skills, not to mention left and right brained activities. Lisa would have the opportunity to use both sides of her brain simultaneously.

Their Lisa would use 100% of her brain power, and not 2%, as most statistics suggest that the average person uses on a daily basis. The Wealth Center continued this Implementation for less than one year, up to the time she began walking, which was earlier than other children her age.

When placed in a room with children her own age, both male and female, Lisa could without question, outperform them, even in play. Lisa had Excelled all the other children who had been pre-selected to be a part of The Wealth Study.

Once Lisa reached the milestone when she had said her first words, visual aids were used as The Wealth Center produced more and more visual images and words that flashed across the screen as Lisa stared off and on at the television during playtime.

Magazines would be shown to Lisa that highlighted fashion savvy, Wealthy-Looking architecture, Wealthy vacation spots, Wealthy paintings, Wealthy art museums, etcetera. She would be Exposed to hearing new languages and complex mathematical problems. What was the result? She <u>mastered</u> everything that was put in front of her in record time. Dr. Wells deemed their Lisa a "GIFTED CHILD," and recommended further testing to test her cognitive and social skills.

Meanwhile, Lisa was still being <u>S</u>aturated with Stories and Tapes of Health and Wealth. <u>She was starting to Recite Stories of her own that were Far More Advanced than what she had been listening to.</u> Her acute ability to listen was greatly sharpened. The Wealth Center was delighted with Lisa's Progress. The Wealth Programming was working. These major findings would benefit millions of families locally, regionally, nationally, and internationally. This was the scientific breakthrough that everyone at The Wealth Center had been hoping for.

By the time Lisa got to 1ˢᵗ grade, she was already ahead of the other students. She was reading at a 7ᵗʰ grade level. Because Lisa was at The Wealth Center, rather than being held back to wait on her classmates to catch up to her, and rather than being placed too prematurely in a higher grade that might stunt her social development, Lisa was allowed to spend a part of the day with her own private Wealth Tutor and Governess, Anna. Anna was to allow Lisa to engage in activities that encouraged her freedom of thought, freedom of expression, and natural curiosity for the world around her. While other students were learning Spanish and French, Lisa was studying the cultures of the languages she had already learned.

While other students were learning how to do multiplication and division, Lisa was solving financials problems most Corporate Executive Officers could not fathom. While other students were learning about geography, Lisa was <u>designing plans</u> for raising funds for multiple world organizations. While other students were studying politics, <u>Lisa was conversing with</u> <u>Prime Ministers during world summits!</u>

Lisa was the only student in the class with a passport. The whole purpose of this Study was to Open Doors that Lisa's successors could easily walk through. Yet, despite such an Advanced Regimen of Study, during lunch period, Lisa enjoyed eating peanut butter and jelly sandwiches with her friends. <u>She absolutely adored recess!!!</u>

During summer breaks, Lisa would accompany her mom and dad to various cities and countries worldwide. No matter where she went, she would never forget to listen to her Health and Wealth

Tapes. Someone was always available to Read Stories of Wealth to her. Lisa was at the point where she would Read these same stories to anyone who wanted to hear about <u>How Easy It Is To Attract Wealth!!!</u>

Lisa knew that Wealth Was Her Birthright, and she wore that Wealth very well. She was so Full of Wealth, there could never be anything less!!! All Lisa's life, even from her mother's womb, she had learned about the importance of tithing (giving 1/10 of everything God gives you back to Him). She had been taught about the importance of Planting and Sowing Seeds Of Wealth. For Lisa, Sowing Money Seeds and Wealth Seeds <u>yielded a multitude of Never-Ending Wealth Harvests and Money Harvests.</u>

At the age of 16, Lisa was selected by The Wealth Center to represent them Nationally and Internationally for one year as an Ambassador of Wealth. She was scheduled to travel to the most impoverished countries of the world to <u>Speak Forth Wealth</u> and to <u>Pronounce A Blessing</u> over every citizen in every community. She literally, took Wealth to the whole world and to all nations because her mom, dad, and The Wealth Center staff Programmed Her For Wealth before Birth. She became the Poster Child Of Wealth.

Upon completing her assignment as an Ambassador of Wealth, The Wealth Center gave Lisa the opportunity to pursue a dual Ph.D in Psychology and Astronomy. The whole world is

Full Of Wealth that God Created and Lisa wanted to share that knowledge with everyone around the globe. <u>She wanted everyone to know that if you have a Wealthy Mentality, you can Experience A Level of Wealth that has yet to be tapped into.</u>

Chapter Seventeen

The More Perfect Union

Lisa never left The Wealth Center. During her travels, she met and married her Soul Mate, Dr. Christian Yahweh Wright. Christian and Lisa had originally met in Nairobi, Kenya three summers ago when she was hosting an international summit on Spiritual Subliminal Programming, Biblical Meditation and their immediate impact on <u>Prenatal and Genetic Imprinting</u>.

For her own reference, she wanted to know what would happen if a child, teenager, or adult who had not participated in The Wealth Study used the same Principles she had been <u>Exposed To</u>, beginning in her Mother's Womb. Could each of these individuals modify, reprogram, if not completely change his or her DNA and Genetic Makeup? Was what she had learned all these years just "in the Genes?" What was the relationship between Subliminal Programming and

Genetic Structuring, if any? If the answers to these <u>thought-provoking</u>, <u>trend-setting questions</u> were, "Yes," such knowledge could have a PROFOUND IMPACT on the total infrastructure of Subliminal Programming and Education.

Christian, a devout Christian and Creationist, was a scientist by profession. He held a Bachelor's Degree in Biology, A Master's degree in Biology and Genetics, as well as a Doctorate in Biology and Genetics. Presently, he was in Nairobi, Kenya putting together a documentary to satisfy the requirements for his second Doctorate – an Ed.D. He was also a best-selling author, lecturer, and an avid fan of Public Policy!

Like Lisa, Christian had an IQ of 450 and a never-ending curiosity of the world he lived in. He would, every second of the rest of his earthly Life, explore every area of interest from every possible angle.

Lisa had no idea that Christian and his family, had also been selected to participate in the Wealth Study. Unlike Mary and Jason, who had elected to stay at the Wealth Center permanently, Christian and his parents had moved back to London, England two weeks before Mary and Jason had moved in. Christian had wanted to explore other options that were now open to him as a Result of the Study.

From the very start, Christian had excelled in all his Programming. He had always been fascinated with the biological side of The Wealth

Study, and how his acquired knowledge had come into fruition. Was it a miracle? Was it associated with cell development or molecular structure? Was it just Subliminal Programming? Did it have anything to do with neurobiology? One way or another he would combine his love for biology and education to find an answer to that question. The world would want to know. He wanted to know.

Of course, that was not all he wanted to know! He was absolutely mesmerized by Dr. Lisa Lee Chancellor. She too was seeking answers about the role The Wealth Center had played in her life, and he was eager to get to know her better. The moment they met, there had been an instant attraction that went deeper than a sexual relationship. They wished everyone could have this kind of experience – one of mutual respect!

Lisa and Christian had exhibited a Meeting of the Minds, <u>Yahweh</u> Style, which was why Christian bore his middle name. He was so named to Instill in him the Power and Blessings of doing everything God's way, or no way at all.

With respect to minds, no one knew the burden of anyone who subjected himself or herself daily, 24 hours a day 7 days a week, to such a Rigorous Subliminal Programming. Once you <u>mastered</u> the Techniques, you became the Technique you were applying daily. It was a nuisance, if not a bother, to have a meaningful, deep conversation with anyone who had not spent as much time in Deliberately trying to Program his or her mind for Massive Wealth.

Lisa was just what he had been looking for all his life, and he was determined that in time, they would spend the rest of their lives together doing what they had been Programmed to do – to be Infinitely Wealthy on every Natural and Supernatural Plane, and not just in terms of Money or Massive Swiss Bank Accounts as people would automatically assume about the Wealthy. Wealth is so much more!

Lisa had been <u>Magnetically</u> <u>Drawn</u> to Christian as well at first glance, and she too wanted to explore Christian's psyche further. As far as she was concerned, Christian was <u>Perfect For Her</u>. <u>He was her Soul Mate</u>. Every time she looked at Christian, she felt as if she was staring into her own soul. They were <u>Equally Yoked</u> in every aspect – M<u>ind, Body, Soul and Spirit</u>. Lisa was fascinated with what she and Christian had in common, academically, mentally, emotionally, physically, financially, socially and Spiritually. Intimately, they both even wanted to wait for their wedding night to consummate their love appropriately and Biblically. Lisa was still a Virgin!!!

It was no surprise to anyone when Christian flew all the way to Hawaii to propose to Lisa while she was visiting family. After all, Hawaii was the next best thing to Paradise On Earth, and there was plenty of natural beauty to explore! Once they married, Lisa and Christian would purchase a vacation home and beach front property in Hawaii to be as close to nature as they could.

Lisa and Christian would <u>live happily ever after</u> in God's Exquisitely Beautiful Creation, and they owed it all to Dr. Joseph Winslow's Wealth Study, which opened their Subconscious Minds to the Infinite Wealth that has always existed in Massive Abundance. Lisa never intended to move out of The Wealth Center. It had been her home – her safe haven – her inner strength. But when she was chosen to assume the position as the next Wealth Center's Director and President, she gladly accepted!!! She and Christian decided they would move the operations to Hawaii where <u>they would take the Wealth Programming to the Ultimate Dimension!</u>

At least then, Christian could pursue his passion for biology, genetics, and love for the natural sciences, while at the same time Taking Full Advantage of Hawaii's natural splendor. Hawaii was the most beautiful place on earth, and it was the perfect place for Lisa to lead the Wealth Study into <u>Higher Dimensions Of Thought</u>, which would allow its participants to Acquire Wealth In Greater Proportions than any previous protégé, including she and Christian. <u>They considered what they had learned at The Wealth Center, before and after birth, as only a Baseline. There was so much more that could and would be accomplished!!!</u>

For example, both Christian and Lisa had spent their whole lives <u>Deliberately Programming Their Minds for Infinite Wealth</u>. They both represented The Wealth Center very well as Ambassadors of Wealth. There had been a lot of traveling across America and across continents. There had been little time for leisure, except on family vacations.

For that reason, Lisa, would, once the operations were moved to Hawaii, use her Expertise Of The Program to <u>Design</u> much more fun ways of Programming. Participants would be required to spend hours on end exploring the islands while at the same time engaging in Biblical Meditation and Subliminal Programming. Meditation Classes would be held outdoors. Tapes she used to listen to at night could be enjoyed by her participants as they basked in Hawaii's sun, taking in the beauty of their surroundings. The Programming had been good to her, but as Lovers of God's Universe, she and Christian felt that Hawaii's being the most beautiful place in the world would yield its participants <u>Greater Wealth in less time, with less effort</u>. They would take the concept of "World Summit" to another level. Pretty soon, such a Phenomenon would catch on and everyone would discover that these Remarkable Teachings Could Be Implemented in the privacy of one's own home, and they would be fully adaptable to fit any desired goal or lifestyle change.

Her mom and dad were delighted that Lisa had found her Mr. Right (Wright)! They had, in keeping with the United States Constitution, "Formed A More Perfect Union!" <u>They were perfect alone, but they would be even more perfect together as husband and wife!</u>

Lisa and Christian were married in London, England and out of their Perfect Union, Hannah Lynn Wright was born. The Wealth Center staff was pleased with this marriage! First of all, it was the first time in The Wealth Center's history that two Wealth Center protégés had decided to marry.

Secondly, their marriage only proved to The Wealth Center staff that their induction of Wealth Study Participants from all walks of life, no matter where they previously resided in the world, was successful. These <u>Strategies would work for Anyone, Anywhere, Anytime, if he or she took the time to Work The Principles!</u> They had proven the theory that Infinite Wealth is not reserved only for a "select few." Many might think that such Infinite Wealth is only a fairytale. <u>But Mary, Jason, Lisa, and Christian had proved that fairytales do come true! Not through wishful thinking, or dreaming, but by setting one's destiny by Deliberately Changing The Thoughts He or She Thinks</u>, which is what Biblical Programming actually is – <u>Thinking The Thoughts Of God Daily</u>!!!

Together, Christian and Lisa are now running The Wealth Center, as they <u>Deliberately Instill in their daughter</u>, Hannah, All The Wealth that had been Instilled in them from birth. <u>As everyone expected, Hannah broke every milestone her mom and dad had accomplished. She made them look like amateurs!!!</u>

Epilogue

Mary looked absolutely stunning as she walked down the aisle of the large cathedral located in Lake Geneva. All the wedding guests gasped loudly as they feasted their eyes on Mary's long, flowing white chiffon wedding gown, laced and drenched in sparkling diamonds bright enough to leave a transparently visual hologram of a rainbow.

Her long-length diamond studded earrings and necklace brought out the natural sparkle of her beautiful brown eyes. Everyone could notice how well the yellow gold in her wedding veil's tiara (made especially for her) complemented the Gold pearls on her lovely white shoes, which she proudly wore to simulate walking down the Streets Of Gold in Heaven and standing at the Pearly Gates. Mary was an Ambassador of Wealth in her own right.

The moment Mary reached the altar, she realized how Blessed she was! Standing next to her, dressed in his handsome white tuxedo and solid gold shirt was the man of her dreams – The Love Of Her Life – the man who loved her enough to give her the wedding of her dreams in this cathedral – the church that was always a part of Jason's Christian faith – the church that embraced their undying love for one another. This time around, <u>they could afford to have their wedding in this special place</u>, instead of having to get married at town hall by the justice of the peace.

After exchanging their wedding vows that they wrote, as well as their wedding rings, kisses, and "I do's," Mary and Jason could not wait to get to their knock out reception, in which the menu consisted of everything Mary wanted during her first wedding ceremony - everything from A To Z. They also could not wait to take Mary's fairytale ending to another notch. Jason was taking his darling wife on her first visit to Hawaii where they would spend one month honeymooning in the most beautiful place in the world!

With respect to The Wealth Center, all the long-standing research finally paid off in more ways than one!!! The Wealth Study with Lisa went over in such a BIG and GIGANTIC way, The Wealth Center opened its doors, its research facilities, and its Research Methodologies to the public via a month-long "Open house."

World renowned educational consultants, educators, parent resource centers, day care *centers, human and social service agencies, psychologists, child psychologists, prenatal care specialists, OB-GYN's, criminal justice officers, ministers, pastors, youth leaders, financial planners, job resource centers, employment specialists, Wealth Specialists, reading specialists, librarians, and parents were all invited to tour the facilities and participate in seminars, forums, documentaries, and press conferences which were designed to spark human interest in the human mind and how <u>its hidden, innate powers could be fully maximized</u> <u>on a scale unheard of by the world</u>.*

The media from all around the globe was cordially invited to come witness this Unparalleled and Unprecedented World Summit in the effort of "breaking the story."

Major television networks were given the green light to carry the broadcast "live" to every house on every continent. The Wealth Center paid Billions of dollars to buy major airtime and run commercials on television to reach the heart of everyone who wanted to give themselves and/or their loved ones a <u>Head Start</u> in life with Subliminal Wealth Techniques, which could be adapted and modified to fit whatever goal(s) and objective(s) each person wanted to call upon.

The World Summit became such a "buzz," until every magazine and newspaper editor around the world wanted to cover such an amazing event – all of whom desired to feature the coverage as "The top story of the century." Radio talk show hosts were also adamant about conducting interviews "live" as well as "getting the word out." Everyone agreed that such a <u>Phenomenon should be made affordable to everyone who wanted in on such an amazing gift.</u>

Dr. Joseph Winslow's dream of combining cognitive therapy, psychology, child psychology, research, and human growth and development with the Power of Programming The Subconscious Mind was an instant success. Individualized Education Plans, Subliminal Audios, CD's, DVD's, Instructional Materials, Visual Aids, Educational Kits, and more were developed in Massive quantities as a Baseline to assist everyone from single moms to the average citizen in applying these Universal Truths and Principles and adapting them to any Environment to achieve <u>Life-Long Wealth</u> *or any other imaginable goals and objectives.*

All across the country, these educational aids were being employed with <u>Great Success</u>. *Families living in poverty-stricken homes became High-Income families of the Highest Degree. Below average students went on to graduate from Ivy League Universities such as Harvard, Yale, Stanford, and Cornell University. Failing businesses became Trillion dollar industries.* <u>Unborn fetuses</u> *were born with IQ's of 450 or Better, as well as Uncommon Physical Characteristics Deliberately Instilled in them by their parents who used Subliminal Programming regularly.*

*Head Start Programs and Pre-School
administrators had to scramble to Adopt and
Implement <u>Standardized Curriculum Strategies
And Methodologies</u> to keep up with each student's
success. Why? Each student's comprehension
and academic skills, even at the Pre-School
age, was <u>7 to 8 grade levels above the norm and
the national average.</u> Also on the same token,
Reading Specialists had to move quickly with
God- Speed as well as <u>super-human speed</u> to
Accommodate elementary students who were
<u>Reading beyond a high school and college level.</u>*

*As a result, school boards and every
other board had to meet on a regular basis to
revamp their Master's Program for teachers in
Kindergarten through College level (K-College).
Parents and Teachers' Association Meetings
all across the country were holding sessions
constantly to assist parents in their attempts to
help their children with homework. Everyone
needed to keep up with all these academic
demands, <u>ground-breaking, and trend-setting
instruction.</u>*

*Everyone was thinking outside the box. Every
child, regardless of his or her ethnic and socio-
economic background had an <u>Equal Opportunity
to succeed</u> using these Strategies that have
always been in existence since the beginning of
time.*

*Remember the laptop in The Birthing Room
the day Lisa was born on Friday, October 13th?
That technology was not wasted. Every night*

since being at The Wealth Center, Mary had never gone to bed without writing in her Gold journal. She captured every single feeling, emotion, thought, and experience of being at The Wealth Center on paper, which she turned into memoirs. She published those memoirs and her Autobiography became an instant hit. Her book was on the Best Seller list for seven consecutive years in a row!!! She even received multiple movie deals, nationally and internationally.

Mary] went on to get her Bachelor's Degree in Early Childhood Education, a Master of Arts (MAEd) and a Doctorate in Education (EdD), both in a Concentration in Teaching and Learning, and a second Doctorate (Ph.D) in Human Growth and Development. Mary had developed a passion and a knack for devising curricula. She wanted to become an Educational Consultant, an Instructional Specialist, a Mentor to teachers, a Curriculum Supervisor, and ultimately, an Academic Dean, so she could pass this amazing Gift of Knowledge on to future educators.

Jason was so great in his artistic expression of capturing the essence of anything on canvas, he landed a teaching position at a major Art Institute. In due course, he spent so much time capturing Romanticism on canvas, he was encouraged to pursue a double Master's in Fine Arts and Marriage Counseling.

Jason has aspirations of pursuing his Doctorate (he does not know in what), but he may have to enroll in an online Doctorate Program.

Mary, his beloved wife, is four weeks pregnant and is expecting twin boys – Michael Anthony and Mark Anthony - on July 9. Mary and Jason have already been asked to once again <u>Participate</u> in the Wealth Study. Everyone is waiting to see what is on the horizon! How will The Wealth Study play out for the two twin boys that are now on the way?

Other Books By Lisa Lee Hairston

The Infinite Rules To Money

The number one rule to money is that you cannot have a lot of money if you refuse to say the right things about it. You cannot talk broke and expect to become rich! It is absolutely impossible to talk rich and stay broke! You cannot reach the palace talking like a peasant. You cannot talk like a loser and become a winner. What you say about money, and what you say when you talk about money, on a regular and consistent basis will determine how much money you will attract into your life. Follow these Infinite Rules To Money and you can become an astronomical money magnet!!!

Victoria Has A Secret

Joshua gave her a tour of his new home. The exquisite beauty contained within every room and every square inch of Joshua's abode took Victoria's breath away. She was in awe of all the beauty she was taking in at that moment. This was not just any kind of beauty. This beauty was real - the kind of beauty that could not be

compared to her own beauty – which she had
come to think of as superficial.

You Are A Jewel

You are a Daughter of the Most High God.
You are an Heir[ess] of God and a Joint-Heir[ess]
with Christ according to Romans 8:17. Everything
God has – Everything Christ has – Everything
the Holy Ghost has – Everything the whole
kingdom has – belongs to you. That fact alone
makes you an Heir[ess] of the highest degree.
You can go anywhere and do anything God
has called you to be, and He calls you rich! No
exceptions!!! Nothing is impossible unto you if
you believe. No matter how much it costs, God
can afford to lavish you with all his riches!!! Get
used to being rich!!! Get used to living in luxury!!!
You are absolutely a rich woman!!!

The Hallelujah Girl

So, you probably can see why everyone
called Lisa The Hallelujah Girl. Lisa did not do
anything, say anything, go anywhere, or talk to
anyone until she said, "Hallelujah!," first. But,
what most individuals did not know is that Lisa
did not just say, "Hallelujah!" out loud. She said,
"Hallelujah!" silently, twenty-four hours a day,
seven days a week, three hundred and sixty-five
days of the year – three hundred and sixty-six
days in leap year.